The
Truth
about
Spiritual
Phenomena

IRH Press

BOOKS
IRH PRESS
New York

ISBN: 978-1-958655-09-2
Cover Image: HomeArt/Shutterstock.com

Printed in Canada

First Edition

LIFE'S Q&A
with
EL CANTARE

The
Truth
about
Spiritual
Phenomena

RYUHO OKAWA

IRH PRESS

Contents

Preface 13

CHAPTER TWO

Freeing Yourself from Spiritual Disturbances

CHAPTER THREE

How to Overcome Spiritual Sensitivity

CHAPTER FOUR

Spread the Truth and Save the People

Afterword

Preface

This is a collection of the Q&A sessions from my earlier lectures and seminars that were held between the second and sixth years of Happy Science. In this volume, I mainly focus on how to deal with spiritual phenomena and spiritual disturbances.

In truth, it is not easy to answer these kinds of questions using simple language.

Although it has been nearly 30 years since I held those Q&A sessions, I can still publish them without changing their content. This proves that the content of this book is universal and eternal, making it a fundamental textbook on spiritual disturbances and the like.

I believe that many people are experiencing various spiritual phenomena or are becoming more spiritually sensitive. So I ask you to please read this book whenever you feel the need to do so.

Also, I would like to emphasize the importance of faith, which I could not cover enough in this book. Please believe in me. People who become "mini-gods" and refuse to listen to others are beyond help.

Ryuho Okawa
Master & CEO of Happy Science Group
September 28, 2021

CHAPTER ONE

Understanding
Spiritual Phenomena
That Occur Near You

1

There Are Three Meanings to Your Dreams

Q1

I am not a member of Happy Science yet. Jesus Christ and other high spirits appear in my dreams, and they teach me how to discipline my mind and offer guidance on how to live my life. I am baffled by these dreams and am not sure what to think of them. Are they genuine or delusional dreams? Or is my guardian spirit disguising itself as those high spirits and appearing in my dreams?

The Seventh Public Lecture of 1989, "Rediscovering the Eightfold Path," held on October 8, 1989, at Marugame Civic Center in Kagawa, Japan

When high spirits appear in your dreams

OK, here is my answer.

There are three kinds of dreams people have when they are sleeping.

The first one is an astral projection. This is where your soul leaves your physical body and travels to the Spirit

World. Your soul perceives what you experience in the Spirit World as it is. This is one type.

The second one is, as you mentioned, when your guardian spirit or guiding spirit shows you visions in your dreams for certain reasons. This is the second type.

The third type is the visualization of your strong desires. Sometimes, the images you vividly uphold in your mind or things you strongly wish for manifest visually in your dreams. These are the three types.

Have I not appeared in your dreams yet? [*Laughs.*] I have heard from people all over Japan that I appeared in their dreams. I wonder if I am really going around appearing in people's dreams that often, but it seems like that is the case. The third type is linked to people's strong desires. What your soul is ardently seeking is visualized in your dreams.

Based on what you told me, the high spirits in your dreams are spirits of the ninth dimension. However, it is safe to assume that spirits of the ninth dimension never directly appear and talk to people. There may be exceptions, but rarely.

Therefore, I would categorize your situation as the third case. You are strongly seeking religious awakening deep in your soul. This strong yearning is projecting those images into your dreams. This happens now and then, so I think your dreams fit into the third type.

I do not sense any evil spiritual vibrations from talking to you, which is a good sign. I don't think you are being deluded. What is happening is your strong desire is being visualized in your dreams. Of course, some spirits may be assisting you in visualizing your dreams, but I would say you are currently at that level.

Other than that, my suggestion is for you to become a member of Happy Science and further study the Truth. Whether you can really communicate with high spirits or not will become apparent as you study and practice my teachings for a while. So why not give it a try? There are many members who have a deeper understanding of the Truth than you do, and as you interact with them, you will gradually understand whether you can really communicate with high spirits.

At first, many people tend to think of spiritual awakening as an "all or nothing" situation. But in reality, there are steps and stages to spiritual awakening. You must follow each step in the right order. You do not understand this concept enough yet, so please study more and more. That is what I recommend.

2

Judging the Content of Your Inspiration

Q2

I receive visions in the form of dreams, but sometimes I cannot determine whether those inspirations come from my guardian spirit or another being. Could you please teach me how to tell where my inspiration comes from?

Intensive Dharma Seminar for Branch Managers,
"A Lecture on *The Principle of Utopia*,"
held on July 27, 1991, at Hotel Heritage in Saitama, Japan

Make judgments that are appropriate
to your state of mind

You should not excessively rely on outside power in this case.

As you keep reading spiritual messages from high spirits, you will eventually acquire a certain sense, a kind of sense that high spirits have. You will be able to sense things in such a way as you continue to study the Truth.

Then, when you start developing this sense, you will gradually be able to tell the difference between light and darkness. You will be able to tell whether something belongs to darkness or light. When your mind is at peace, you will be able to accurately judge this.

However, you must be careful when you feel very agitated or are under pressure at work. These are certainly dangerous times. That is why you should have a circle of trusted friends you can talk to. In difficult situations, ask those friends, "What do you think of the inspiration I'm getting?"

For example, let's say you consult three Happy Science members who are earnestly studying to become lecturers or who are already lecturers. There is no way all three of them will misjudge the work of evil spirits as the work of your guardian spirit. At least two of them will make the right judgment. So ask them, "What do you think of my current state of mind?" If two or three of them conclude that you are in a good state, you should be all right.

The people you can rely on when you feel unsure of yourself are, indeed, your friends who have been studying the Truth with you. They have been studying with you, so they know. People are unsure of their own decisions when they have something to gain or lose. If you find yourself in such a situation, please seek advice from people who have been studying with you. It is one of the benefits of holding regular group study sessions.

Just ask them frankly. Leave aside your pride. Find someone you trust, ask for their opinions regardless of their qualifications, and listen to their advice. Then you will know. If everyone warns you, you should stop and not take any actions. Give yourself some time, perhaps a week or a month. When you go back to it again, you may realize you were not in the right state of mind.

In this way, a sangha or a group of friends who study the Truth together are incredibly reliable when you are in a dangerous situation or struggling to make the right decision. That is why it is risky to study alone without the support of these friends. Some people say, "I can buy books from the store and read and practice them as I please." They claim, "I do not need to become a member to study. I have access to books and CDs of the lectures. I can study and practice on my own." Unfortunately, those people are nothing but self-styled practitioners.

You can believe in your inspiration when you have no attachments or any major worries and are studying the Truth. But when you feel you are at risk, please ask others for advice. You will get the overall feel by asking three or so people. If all of them tell you to put a hold on your thoughts, it is best not to act on your judgment. Instead, you should focus on your normal day-to-day activities and make steady efforts for a while.

I can only give you a general answer, as the content of a person's inspiration depends on his or her state of mind. But it all comes down to having "self-reliance." You must be able to trust yourself. In other words, you should know your "average marks" of your judgment. It is like analyzing how many marks you can score on a test. It is to know, "I can score 80 points on this test" or "I can get 90 points on this test." It is important to recognize your capability.

If you know how capable you are of solving certain problems, you will have a sense of security. You can remain calm when incidents happen. I would like you to please be aware of your capability. Your score may be 80 or 90 points, and from there, you can gradually increase your score. In this way, you can gradually raise your capability. That is what I recommend.

3

The Workings of Foresight and Gut Feeling

Q3

My question is about when you foresee events in dreams, such as earthquakes or someone getting hurt. And there is also that gut feeling, which I'm sure many people have experienced. Please teach us the workings or principles behind these things.

The 11th Public Lecture of 1990, "The Road toward Enlightenment,"
held on October 7, 1990, at Nagaoka City Kosei Kaikan
in Niigata, Japan

How are this world and the Spirit World related?

It may be easier to find answers to your question by watching a television program on spiritual phenomena rather than seeking them at Happy Science. We have pretty much ignored those things and are taking things much further with our teachings. Indeed, your topic of concern is the starting point and what leads people to take an interest in the other world or in religions.

The thing is, topics related to your question are being covered by countless other people, and you can find many programs featuring them. So I ignored them and went further ahead. I have been teaching about the orderly, structural part of the Spirit World itself. Before this level, you will experience those kinds of phenomena quite often.

Of course, you may sometimes foresee events or have a gut feeling as a result of spiritual inspiration. This is because every event that occurs in this world has already occurred in the Spirit World; it actually occurs a little earlier in the Spirit World. It is like looking at a film reel, where you can sort of tell what will show on the screen in the next scene. When the image is projected onto the screen, the event takes place in the three-dimensional world. This is why most events that occur in this world can be seen as having already occurred in the Spirit World.

People foresee things or have gut feelings in one of two ways. One is when they sense something through their spiritual abilities or spiritual experiences. Another is when they are informed by someone else. A gut feeling quite often means that someone who is about to die or has just died has come to tell you something. For example, the spirit body of a person nearing his or her death begins to leave the physical body two or three days before their death. The spirit body goes in and out of the physical body. Then the people around them, such as their friends or family, often sense signs of the person's death. So when you are nearing death, your soul can sometimes visit other people to inform them about it before it happens.

I am starting to get the chills, so let's end it here. Today is a hot day, but now it is getting chilly, so we will end it here. Anyhow, such things can happen. That will be all for now.

4

Spiritual Influence of Land and Houses

Q4

Can people who know and study the Truth live in a spiritually defiled house or on land near burial grounds or shrines and remain unaffected by them? Or will living in these places slow them down in their study of the Truth, making it difficult for them to attain enlightenment? Please teach us.

The Third Public Lecture of 1989, "Secrets of the Multidimensional Universe," held on May 28, 1989, at Kobe Port Island Hall in Hyogo, Japan

---

Cautions concerning spiritual fields and how to improve them

OK. Here is my answer from two perspectives.

First, I will answer from a wider point of view—regarding the evolution of the soul. I do not think there is any particular effect of staying near certain locations on the evolution of your soul. The environment will help you make spiritual progress regardless of whether it is good or bad. This is from the macro perspective.

Of course, things will be different from a micro perspective—in other words, an individual's perspective. For example, can an enlightened person be comfortable in any spiritual environment? What do you think?

Right now, I am giving this lecture at a newly built event hall. But what if I held this lecture at a graveyard? Would you all feel comfortable? I think most of you will feel somewhat unpleasant. That is the reality. Spiritual fields certainly do exist.

Also, there is a limit to how much an individual can remain unaffected by spiritual fields. For instance, a sound, energetic person with an unclouded mind can keep his state of mind even if someone near him is possessed by two or three evil spirits. But if he is surrounded by five, ten, or twenty people possessed by evil spirits, then unfortunately, he will not be able to maintain his state of mind. The influence of evil spirits is too strong. As the saying goes, "He who touches pitch shall be defiled." If you are surrounded by that many evil spirits all the time, you will certainly be under a bad influence. It may lead to a decline in your health, or you may become emotionally unstable. This depends on each person's capacity. There is only so much a person can handle alone.

Another point is that there are still places like the "Devil's Mansion" in modern times. Let me refer to one of the questions I received in a Q&A session that was held at our training facility in Tokyo. The question came from a man who had rented his house to someone for two years. But it turned out he made a huge mistake; his tenant was a cult leader. When his house was returned to him, his entire family fell sick, and they could not recover.

To answer his question, I did a spiritual reading on the house and found that the house had become a den of evil spirits. Because the cult leader lived there, the house itself became a nest or shrine of evil spirits. The person who asked the question then asked if he could repel them by reading books of Happy Science and playing CDs of my lectures. But my answer was that he did not have enough power to get through it; the mass gathering of evil spirits would overpower him. I told him to move out because the situation was too severe and his life would be in danger by staying there.

There are evil spiritual fields like that and, the point is, each person has a limit to how much he or she can withstand. If you cannot cope with the situation alone, then you should join hands with many people. Even if the spiritual field is an evil one, if plenty of people with harmonized minds get together, it will change. But if there aren't enough harmonized people, you will gradually fall under such evil influences. That is how it goes.

This was an example of a spiritual field on a small scale. On a bigger scale, there are many unclean spiritual fields everywhere across Japan. To improve it, my power alone is not enough. It simply won't be enough. Instead, we need many people who emit light to appear. As more and more people who are filled with light appear across the country, the darkness will gradually disappear. That is the way.

Did you understand my explanation? In conclusion, I advise you to avoid locations or houses with negative spiritual fields. This is my answer at the individual level. However, on the macro level, you can turn any circumstance into a springboard for enlightenment. That is my answer.

5

Advice for People with an Interest in Fortune-Telling

Q5

You taught us that fortune-telling and the like belong in the Sennin (Hermit) Realm of Rear Heaven. But I think *I Ching*, or the Chinese book of divination, is something of a higher level. Can you please teach us its origin and the level of its philosophy?

The Sixth Public Lecture of 1989, "The Way to Human Perfection,"
held on August 6, 1989, at Sapporo Education and Culture Hall in Hokkaido, Japan

---

The most common way of thinking that makes people happy

Happy Science has been intentionally avoiding the topics of divination, fortune-telling, and destiny. But that does not necessarily mean they are all completely wrong. You may consider them the collective wisdom of those who lived before us. These people have thought hard and sought ways to shape their destinies and attain happiness. The spirits who spiritually guide different forms of divination might get angry if people say they have no love or mercy. They have their own theory of happiness, and based on it, they built methods to make people happy in various ways. They could teach what are lucky and unlucky directions, dates, and names for you. So those involved in divination do not think they lack love or mercy.

Nonetheless, I must mention the following.

There are many different ways to make people happy, so we cannot limit it to a single way. However, you can also say there is a common way of thinking that makes people happy—a common way of thinking that has stood the test of thousands, tens of thousands, or even more years. I belong to the majority or the mainstream spirit group that teaches this philosophy. We teach, "What makes people happy or unhappy depends on their mindset. You can shape your destiny with your mindset." This is because your soul will develop by thinking in this way. Your soul will make greater progress.

Simply changing your name or choosing locations or routes will not truly awaken your soul.

People who misuse divination or fortune-telling tend to believe that others will harm them. They avoid anything that could potentially harm them and think about securing their safety zone. These kinds of thoughts are different from thoughts of love. They are not thoughts about making the world and others better but rather self-preserving thoughts. This way of thinking is a little narrow-minded, and that is why they belong to Rear Heaven.

If these people could broaden their love, they would be better off, but they are too focused on warding off misfortune and evil. This is a narrow way of thinking. Because of this, they cannot make up the majority.

But here is the positive side to this way of thinking. It is true that you can somewhat predict people's destinies. There are scientists in the Spirit World who can foresee the different scenarios people may face in the future. So there is indeed a small field of divination in spiritual science.

I will not stop you from feeling especially drawn to this type of divination. But I prefer to adopt the commonly accepted thinking learned from past examples—in other words, the majority's way of thinking.

What to keep in mind
regarding divination and fortune-telling

If you have a keen interest in divination or fortune-telling and wish to study them, please be careful when doing it for others. Many of those who practice these things go to hell.

They are the ones who speak negatively about everything. In fact, most people who make money out of divination or fortune-telling are like that.

They see your future and speak badly of it. For example, they will say, "You are in danger. Watch out. Beware. In the future, you will get into an accident and end up like this." They stir up fear in you and make money out of it. This kind of business is dangerous, so you must be careful.

Only a few fortune-tellers tell you good things. I would say less than 10 percent. If they truly want to make people's lives better, their warmhearted thoughts belong to heaven. But those who emit negative thoughts and imply a bad future are very likely to fall to hell.

I myself have investigated them before. If you go to Asakusa, you will see many fortune-tellers lined up on the street. Once, a long time ago, I went around asking them about my future. In a way, I was challenging them.

I let them freely speak about various things. Unfortunately for them, I knew who was sending them inspiration and what those spirits were saying. I could tell. I saw through everything, like who was saying what. I could tell as I was observing them, but it was not a pleasant experience.

In most cases, they reminded me of amphibians and reptiles. These spirits gave off a slimy, grim, cold feeling. It was as if I had touched a frog. Encounters with such spirits will leave you with a truly unpleasant aftertaste.

They are a little different from the spirits in hell. They aren't the same; I'm not sure how to describe it. It was as if I was in a shabby house with raindrops leaking through the roof. It was that kind of feeling. It did not feel right. It felt very uncomfortable. This means that fortune-tellers share this kind of soul tendency.

I would just like you to know the facts. That is all.

6

The Spiritual Effect of Advertisements and Commercials

Q6

I have not been able to study the teachings in an organized way, so please teach me. I have heard about *genrei-gaku* (the study of words with spiritual power) before, and I want to ask you about the spiritual power of words and how it relates to the human subconsciousness.

I run a company called "Give and Give." When my business grows, I want to use TV advertisements to send out the message, "For the world, for the people, and for yourself," by spreading my company name, "Give and Give." Although it may be small, I hope this action will help improve the world of hell and bring light to the human consciousness. I would be so grateful if you could give me advice on this.

I think the most definite way to change humanity is by having people read and understand the books of Truth. But my question is, will people's consciousness change if I continuously send out words like "Love" and "Give and Give," without much explanation, in mass media such as newspapers?

The Seventh Public Lecture of 1990, "The Declaration of Victory,"
held on July 8, 1990, at Morioka City Ice Arena in Iwate, Japan

One of the greatest tools
the angels of light use to guide people

The first part of your question is whether there is a connection between *genrei* or *kotodama* (the spiritual power of words) and the history of humankind. Nowadays, there are many books about the spiritual world out there in society; but their quality varies, and the contents are all jumbled. So we should not consider such spiritual knowledge to be all on the same level. But genrei-gaku is a little different.

When the angels of light guide and teach people, they always use words. Since ancient times, Japanese people have believed in kotodama or the spiritual power of words. Words have their own vibrations, and they can be grouped into good words and bad words.

For example, take the word "hate." It is not a very nice word. If you ask someone to tell you "I hate you" several times, even as a joke, you will not be able to stand it. On the other hand, if someone tells you "I love you" or "You are such a wonderful person," you will become very happy. This is because words themselves have tremendous power.

People speak different languages depending on their country. In the Spirit World, spirits up to a certain level also speak their own languages, but when it comes to the angels of light, there is virtually no language barrier. They communicate through thoughts and ideas.

Thoughts come first. These thoughts are then translated into words that we use in this world. Therefore, each word is filled with a certain vibration.

Now, let us look at the actual words. For example, there is the Bible. If you extract Jesus' words and exclude all background descriptions in the Bible, they would only amount to a few dozen pages. However, his very words contain strong power and light. The light that is emitted from Jesus' words makes its way into people's hearts and touches them. In this way, words have tremendous power.

Words—or the spiritual power of words—are one of the greatest tools that the angels of light use to guide people. That is why all religious leaders are poets.

They have poetic souls. Whether it be Jesus or Nichiren, they are all poets. There is spiritual power in their words.

Only a few are allowed to know the past, present, and future of humanity

Your other question about human history is a different story altogether. I cannot speak about it too much because it will be a long story.

But I can tell you that spirits above a certain realm are given information about the past, present, and future of humanity. They are able to see past events as well.

These spirits are usually at the level of tathagatas and above. It is rare for bodhisattvas to get involved in such matters. Bodhisattvas, through their mentors, will only be given this information if and when it is necessary. Otherwise, they will not be told.

To be even more precise, the spirits in the upper realm of the eighth dimension, known as the Sun Realm, and above are allowed to know about and discuss the secrets of human history. The spirits below them may have vaguely heard about this information but cannot clearly speak about it.

Spiritually awakened people perceive the media differently

When you asked your question, you seemed so reserved in saying "without much explanation." But as I have just mentioned above, words have meanings, of course.

So when spiritually awakened people watch the news or read the newspaper, they perceive it differently from ordinary, unawakened people. For example, sadly, I cannot watch an entire news program on TV, such as the six o'clock or seven o'clock news. That is because the news always contains homicides. It shows clips of comments and interviews as well as crime scenes. The images leave me with deep pain, so I cannot bear to watch.

The same goes for words. People speak about all kinds of things, but I cannot listen to them for long when they start speaking words with very negative vibrations.

Furthermore, I cannot watch people who appear on TV that are possessed by many evil spirits. This is often the case for politicians. Sometimes, you will see politicians holding panel discussions on TV, but those are very hard for me to watch. I cannot watch or listen to people who are possessed by horrible beings. That is how it is.

As you can see, words are used to speak and express yourself. But I must say, your words express the thoughts within you; they speak of your true nature. Once they are written out as printed letters, other people may not know what is in your mind, but they are most definitely connected to the thoughts you have in your mind.

The media makes a connection to your mind. Whether it is in the form of a TV program, a newspaper article, or a flyer, it connects to your state of mind. In addition, people who receive your words through the media, in whatever form it may be, will connect to your mind. It is like a phone call.

So the point is not about whether your company name, "Give and Give," has any meaning. What is important is whether you meaningfully believe in the words used in your company name. If you chose the name "Give and Give" because you think it is an interesting name for a company or because you think the company will succeed by giving people the impression that it is helping others, the name will not inspire people. Those words may connect with people's minds but leave them with no impression.

However, if you sincerely hope to run your company for the sake of giving to people, the phrase "Give and Give"—whether it is in the form of writing or an image—will make its way into and awaken people's minds. It is mysterious, indeed. In this case, those words will be meaningful.

To conclude, everything depends on the thoughts you had in the beginning. No matter how much you focus on the words, if your intention is bad, everything will be meaningless. Please think in this way.

So study hard and become a member of Happy Science. Then your words will get better and better.

7

Problems with Misguided Exorcism

Q7

Recently, I experienced a series of unfortunate events, so I received an exorcism at another religion. I also bought a Buddhist altar for my deceased father and older sister.

I know I am completely relying on outside power, but I pray every morning for my wishes to be granted. Right now, I am raising a child by myself, so I am worried about what will happen to us if my wishes do not come true.

I would like to ask how effective exorcisms are and whether wishes can be granted.

The Second Public Lecture of 1989, "The Discovery of Enlightenment," held on March 19, 1989, at Kyusyu Koseinenkin Hall in Fukuoka, Japan

Do exorcisms work?

Whether an exorcism works depends on the power of the person conducting it. Exorcisms are performed across the country, and they will work if the priest conducting them has enough spiritual power. If not, they will not work, of course. Don't you agree? It's a matter of fact.

Therefore, yes, it is true that exorcisms work to an extent if performed by a psychic who can draw on the power of divine spirits.

Let's say you are possessed by an evil spirit. If I scold and tell it to leave, it will. This is also a type of exorcism. But if an ordinary, non-religious person tells it to leave, it won't. The evil spirit will ignore the person completely. That is because an ordinary person cannot tell whether someone is possessed. As for me, I can tell. I am able to tell whether an evil spirit has left the person. If it is still haunting the person, I will preach to it, and then it will leave.

In this way, not being able to tell whether an exorcism has worked means you are most likely scammed. Needless to say, most of the exorcisms performed across the country are not effective. Very few of them are effective; the majority of them are ineffective. In most cases, priests perform exorcisms as a means of making their living.

Imagine that you have died and become a lost spirit. Let's say a Shinto priest comes and swings a wand with white paper, like the ones used in Shinto rituals, in your face. Will you be persuaded to leave? I don't think so. You will most definitely think, "What are you doing?" Will you run away after seeing smoke rise from the burning incense? You won't. You will think, "How dumb are you? I have no physical body, so I can't even smell!" Those rituals are at that level, so they rarely work.

Of course, if the priest conducting the ritual has enough spiritual ability, it will work. But you must remember that the effects of most exorcisms are only temporary. Evil spirits can be expelled momentarily, but they will come back.

For example, if you are possessed temporarily, the problem will be solved once the possessing spirit is expelled. On the other hand, if you have been possessed by the same evil spirit for 10 or 20 years, it means the spirit has already become your "regular customer." You have already developed a connection with it. So you can have it exorcised, but it will keep coming back. Such spirits are like lost dogs that have nowhere else to go. They will trace their way back to their familiar place, their shelter. No matter how many times they are exorcised, they will come back again and again.

In that case, exorcisms will be less effective. If you are temporarily possessed, I can point to the person next to you and say, "Move." The evil spirit will then leave you, and that will be all. But if you have been possessed for a long time, then that is another story.

What is true exorcism?

Now, why do you attract such evil spirits? The cause lies in your mind. The possessing spirits and those who are possessed always have something in common. They are alike. People become possessed because they share something similar with the possessing spirits.

No matter how hard evil spirits try, they cannot possess those who are not like them—in other words, people with spotlessly clean minds. Even if the evil spirits try hard to possess such people, they can only stay with them for a day. It is painful for evil spirits to possess them because they emit light. Possessing spirits cannot influence a person with a harmonized mind for more than a day. They will eventually leave.

Therefore, in the truest sense, exorcism is not about outside power. To truly exorcise evil spirits, you must emit light from within—in other words, from your mind. This is a difficult and tough path but also 100 percent possible for everyone.

You can ask for an exorcism, but how would you know whether the exorcist has power? In most cases, you are probably being scammed. On the contrary, emitting light from within yourself is a path that is available to all.

Once you attain a spotless mind that is free from clouds or dust, you will emit a halo. Light will shine from the back of your head, and evil spirits will not be able to stay with you any longer. Since you are always so radiant and bright, they will have to leave.

The law of the mind always works. It may not be effective immediately, but it is the best approach in the long run.

Do ancestral services work?

I talked about exorcism, but this also relates to memorial services for ancestors. Whether the one conducting the service is a Shinto priest or a Buddhist monk, sutras will have no effect if the ones reciting them are incapable of truly convincing the spirits of the deceased.

Therefore, 99 percent of Japanese monks are, in a way... Please excuse me if there are any monks here today. I will be careful with my words. There is a crime called fraud. It is when you receive monetary rewards under pretense. Memorial services for ancestors have become exactly like this. It is obviously the case.

Most monks are just simply reading the sutra. They cannot connect with spirits or help them return to heaven. So they should only charge a "recitation fee" that accords with their work. If they are charging anything more than that, there is a problem.

On the other hand, the same sutra used for this memorial service will work to a certain level if it is read by someone who understands the meaning or content of it and who emits light from their mind.

Happy Science has the powerful fundamental sutra "The True Words Spoken By Buddha" and "Prayers Book." But in my case, I could also recite the "Heart Sutra" and it will still work (Note 1). This sutra itself contains vibrations to send spirits to heaven, but it also works because I understand the meaning of the sutra. A person who understands the meaning of the sutra and why spirits are unable to return to heaven can convince them to return to the other world.

That is why it is extremely important for the person who recites the sutra to fully understand it. As a prerequisite, you must know about this world and the other world, and you must know why someone is not saved yet. Otherwise, you can recite sutras all you want but they will have little effect.

This is what I can say in general.

The significance of Happy Science sutras

In Happy Science's "Prayers Book I," you will find "Buddha's Teaching: Sutra for Our Ancestors." This sutra contains the teachings of self-reflection that will guide your ancestors to reflect on themselves. As you recite it and pray for your ancestors, I would also like you to reflect on yourself.

Regarding your question about whether Buddhist altars are necessary, the fact that you own one shows that you care for your ancestors; the act of preparing the altar and praying to it shows your feelings for them. This is certainly an act of love (Note 2).

If you are already a member of Happy Science, keep studying the Truth and recite the "Prayers Book." If you have not joined us yet, please become a member and recite the sutra. The more you know the Truth, the stronger the power of your prayer becomes.

I will say that there are many memorial services for ancestors out there that have not yet been investigated for their effect and are not trustworthy.

"The True Words Spoken By Buddha"

"Prayers Book I"

"Prayers Book II"

(Note 1)

Happy Science's fundamental sutra, "The True Words Spoken By Buddha," is a revelation from Shakyamuni Buddha in the heavenly world. It is more than 10,000 times stronger in light and merit than the "Heart Sutra" compiled by the Buddhist disciples of later years. (Refer to the Appendix.)

(Note 2)

Currently, Happy Science followers are allowed to receive the Home Gohonzon and memorial service altars. Memorial services for ancestors, funerals, and other services are held at shojas, at local branches, and at the Happy Afterlife Memorial Park (cemetery).

CHAPTER TWO

Freeing Yourself from Spiritual Disturbances

1

How to Prevent Nightmares

Q1

You taught us that our spirit bodies recharge during our sleep by receiving spiritual energy from the Spiritual Sun. What about when we have bad dreams or dreams of being in hell? Where and how do we get the spiritual energy to recharge ourselves?

The 11th Public Lecture of 1990, "The Road toward Enlightenment," held on October 7, 1990, at Nagaoka City Kosei Kaikan in Niigata, Japan

What you should do before you go to sleep at night

Do you feel refreshed when you wake up after having nightmares? Probably not. You may be tired. You probably wake up sweating and panting. This shows you couldn't receive any spiritual energy.

To tell the truth, when you have nightmares, you are most likely under the influence of hellish spirits. If you had worries and were influenced by multiple evil spirits during the day, and did not self-reflect or clear your mind before going to bed, then you will have nightmares. Spiritual possession by evil spirits is the cause of your nightmares. In most cases, that is the reason.

You might think, "The first level of heaven is a few hundred meters above ground, and the next level is up another few hundred meters," but that is not true. Heaven and hell can exist anywhere; they have nothing to do with physical space or location. You could be in heaven or hell depending on your state of mind.

Therefore, your soul does not aimlessly leave the body and wander. Your soul goes straight to the world that corresponds with the state of your soul. If you are having nightmares, you are already under the influence of evil spirits. This means you are actually visiting hell in your dreams. So if you pay close attention to the surroundings in your dream, you should be able to see horrifying things. You may have many nightmares where you feel threatened for your life and wake up with a big sense of relief that you are alive. These nightmares will seem very real.

I am getting the chills now, so I will not go into it any further. Otherwise, things will turn for the worse. Anyhow, I hope you get the idea.

When you have bad dreams, your soul does not receive light from the Spiritual Sun, so you will still be exhausted after you wake up. If this continues, you will be sleep-deprived, which may cause you to be neurotic. It may get so bad that you cannot work or even sleep at night. Thus, you will be caught in a vicious cycle and eventually become ill or mentally unstable. So you should thoroughly practice self-reflection before you go to sleep at night to avoid having nightmares.

Also, if you feel that there is some spirit near you and that your self-reflection alone is not enough, please listen to my lecture CDs or DVDs for at least 30 minutes before going to sleep. Evil spirits will find it difficult to directly possess you if you do that, so please try it. This is important.

Furthermore, if you are already a member of Happy Science, you should have our fundamental sutra, "The True Words Spoken By Buddha," and "Prayers Book." Please treasure them and recite them daily.

2

Do Not Be Deceived by Evil Spirits

Q2

My question is about the bond between a master and his disciples. I have heard that some people still leave Happy Science even after studying your teachings. Could you please teach us how to strengthen the bond between you and us, the disciples?

The Eighth Public Lecture of 1990, "Living the Eternal Now," held on July 29, 1990, at Aichi Prefectural Gymnasium in Aichi, Japan

How to tell whether a spiritual phenomenon is caused by an evil spirit

Honestly speaking, there are quite a few spiritually sensitive people at Happy Science. Among them are two types of people. One type is those who feel the spiritual vibrations of high spirits and are deeply moved by them. The other type is those under a complete misunderstanding; some spiritually sensitive people are like that. Such people believe they are already connected to and guided by their guardian and guiding spirits. They believe they agree with me or have the same thinking that I do. However, in reality, they are possessed by many evil spirits, and what they think and do are completely different from what I say. These kinds of people exist among Happy Science members. They are just attracted to spiritual things, that is all. They joined Happy Science simply because they like the spiritual world and spirits. But they clearly misunderstand me.

This earthly world is much closer to the fourth dimension than the higher dimensions of the Spirit World. The higher dimensions are very different from this earthly world in terms of spiritual vibration. Spirits of the higher dimensions do not often guide or come down to this world. Instead, spirits of the fourth dimension often influence this world. And hell exists in one region of the fourth dimension, so this earthly world is largely influenced by hell. Many people on earth are affected by the hellish vibrations of the spirits in hell.

There are no issues in the beginning when people are interested in or become sensitive to spiritual things. But gradually, they become influenced by hellish vibrations. Many people are like that. I feel this is somewhat inevitable and cannot be helped, but it shows the harsh reality of getting involved with the spiritual world.

I hear that currently, some Happy Science members are misleading other members by performing spiritual phenomena, which is indeed a problem. Some members follow them believing that being able to perform spiritual phenomena is a wonderful thing. However, that is not entirely true. Although the spiritual phenomena of high spirits are sacred, those of evil spirits are meaningless. They are not even worth a penny, so please do not let such things mislead you.

Therefore, I would like all members to explore Right Mind and study the books of Truth to get a good sense of heavenly vibrations. Once you do, you will get headaches or feel sick when you read or listen to work done by people who are under the influence of evil spirits. You will be able to tell whether something has good or evil vibrations in this way, so please do not think that all spiritual phenomena are sacred.

Suppose there are 100 psychics. About half of them, or 50 percent of them, are fake; they are pretending to be psychics when in truth, they have no spiritual ability. Of the remaining 50, perhaps 47 or 48 are possessed by evil spirits. Evil spirits are aiding them in conducting spiritual phenomena. Only one or two psychics out of 100 are guided by heavenly spirits. This is a realistic number. In nearly all cases, those who claim to be psychics are not guided by heavenly spirits. So please do not get deeply involved with them.

Advice to right-brained people

What should you do to avoid being misled by negative spiritual phenomena? We know that the human brain can be categorized into two halves—the right brain and the left brain. From a spiritual viewpoint, the right side governs the senses and "enlightenment-nature"—in other words, enlightenment. The left side of the brain is related to reason and intelligence. The left brain mostly controls the practical work skills of a person. On the other hand, the right brain, in charge of the senses and enlightenment, is related to one's religious character, sense of literature, and artistic sense.

The soul of an ordinary person is usually small but well-balanced. But among talented people, there are two types: those who excel in reason and intelligence, meaning they are highly capable at work; and those who excel in the senses and enlightenment, meaning they are highly religious and artistic. Those who are right-brained, who have highly developed senses and enlightenment-nature, are easily influenced by spiritual things. If you are heavily inclined toward right-brain tendencies, you may be easily swayed by spiritual phenomena. Just as great artists can have no common sense and act like insane people, you, too could live a life of many ups and downs.

This is a very dangerous way to live, so at Happy Science, I say to everyone that they should aim to become a great person with common sense. I want everyone to make sure they train both the left and right sides of their brain. You can balance the two by strengthening your reason and intelligence and refining your sensibility and enlightenment. Then, they can keep each other in check.

If a person loses this sense of balance to a large degree, he or she will become extremely eccentric and act in a very odd way. A very religious person with weak reason and intelligence will receive all kinds of spiritual vibrations and be led astray by evil spirits, and they will follow them without doubting. This is very dangerous.

Therefore, at Happy Science, we emphasize studying to train your reason and intelligence. If everyone trains themselves to think logically, they can check whether they are under a negative spiritual influence. They will thus be able to repel strange phenomena on their own.

To achieve this state, everyone should begin by becoming studious. There is no end to spiritual phenomena. However, dealing with them too frequently can be very dangerous. Therefore, we must all discipline ourselves by studying hard.

Most people who leave Happy Science are misguided by negative spiritual influences. This world is a border between heaven and hell. We are in a warzone between these two worlds, so some of us will inevitably be hit with "bullets from hell." But there is a way to protect against their attacks. We must gain knowledge and open our eyes to the truth. Then, we will not be lost. Let us remain cautious and pursue Right Mind. We must distinguish right from wrong in light of the Truth. As soon as you waver and have doubts, evil spirits will swiftly move in and wreak havoc. They are always watching us. In a way, they know whom to target. They are trying to prevent the Truth from spreading far and wide because once people learn of the Truth, evil spirits will no longer be able to possess them. It means they will lose their "home." This is why evil spirits are trying to wreak havoc wherever possible. They try to ruin our members' reputations.

However, overall, we are making victories daily. We are making progress year after year. I feel that the Truth is winning.

3

Overcoming Self-Contempt

Q3

Ever since I was young, I tended to belittle myself and suffered feelings of self-contempt. Then, about three years ago, I became very impatient about the fact that I could not overcome my self-contempt. As a result, I put extreme strain on my whole body. Since then, I feel like something physically hard has been possessing the part of my body I particularly despise. I think that I am probably possessed by evil spirits, but I am not sure if this "thing" that began possessing me three years ago is an evil spirit. Can you please reveal what it is from a spiritual point of view?

The Second Special Lecture of 1990, "The Spirit of Missionary Work,"
held on September 2, 1990, at Kitakyushu City Gymnasium in Fukuoka, Japan

---

Why evil spirits can possess people

This is going to be a very considerate "gentleman's answer" to your question, as there are 7,000 people here. So please understand that the answer may not be very straightforward.

Perhaps you already know what I am going to tell you from reading my books. You should not blame the possession for your current condition. It is not very good to think this way for too long. Spiritual possession is not the cause of your problems. There is a set principle that allows spirits to possess you—namely, what has come to possess you relates to your current state of mind. It has to do with the main concern in your mind. Whatever is closest to it has come to you. So if the direction of your mind changes, the evil spirit will not be able to possess you. This is a very clear principle.

It is possible to pour divine light energy into you at once and forcefully remove what is possessing you—in other words, by using outside power. However, everyone has the power to remove evil spirits on their own. It might take a little longer, but once you successfully repel them on your own, you will be able to repel anything that comes your way in the future.

To do this, you must understand what we call the Law of Same Wavelengths' Attraction: you will attract beings with the same wavelength as yours. If your mind is like the mind of an angel, then you will attract an angel. In that case, evil spirits cannot possess you. Only angels will come to you and give you inspiration.

On the contrary, what will happen if your mind continues to be filled with self-contempt? Some angels may be self-contemptuous, but their number is very small, so it is unlikely that you will be visited by angels. What kind of spirits will be attracted to your self-loathing mind? Spirits that match your state of mind will come to you, so in this case, I would imagine a stray spirit of a person who ended their life in self-contempt, disappointment, and agony. Such a spirit will attach itself to you.

Your question did not make much sense—you said you are probably possessed by an evil spirit but were not sure. I think it would be better for you to recognize that you are possessed by an evil spirit. The problem does not lie in the outside factors. Please realize that the problem lies within you. So once your mind becomes merry and cheerful, your problem will go away.

Living a "fine spring day"

The most important thing for people with a sense of self-contempt is to adopt "positive thinking." It will only take a day or two to shift your mindset. Imagine a splendid spring day and maintain the state of mind that echoes such a feeling. This is going to be crucial for you.

It starts with you deciding to have this mindset. Do not think that this is not going to help you or anything negative like that. You must make up your mind to maintain a cheerful, spring-like state of mind. You will see the result almost immediately. As you build a sense of what success feels like, it will become a part of you. It will become second nature to you to be cheerful and lively.

To master this mindset, you should start your day by deciding how to spend it. When you wake up in the morning, you must tell yourself, "I am going to spend today like a fine spring day. Today is going to be a beautiful spring day. I will give everyone I meet today the feeling of fresh, warm spring!" Make a promise to yourself that you will do it. Before you leave the house, look at yourself in the mirror and practice your smile. After you do this for a few days or a week, it will all become very natural to you.

I want to also recommend our series of theory books such as *The Laws of Success* and *Invincible Thinking* to help you maintain a successful mindset in the long term. Please

The Laws of Success
(New York: IRH
Press, 2017)

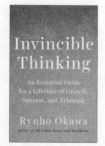

Invincible Thinking
(New York: IRH
Press, 2017)

read these books daily. You will notice the difference within yourself after a week or two. Others around you will also see you differently.

In most cases, people suffer from self-contempt because they are too sensitive about others evaluating them poorly. So the realization of how others change when you change will prompt further changes in you. This will kick off the cycle of positive changes that will lead you in a better direction. When this cycle continues for some time, it will become a part of your ability. Eventually, you will be able to do it at will.

This is definitely possible. Please give it a try. First, you must decide to do it. Never mind what is possessing you. The fact that you are spending time worrying about it already shows that you are straying away from positive thinking. Do not think about it. Begin each day with a fresh start.

4

Getting Out of Serious Spiritual Disturbances

Q4

Currently, I am suffering from a serious case of spiritual disturbance. I used to live in ways that went against the Truth, and I have self-reflected on that part. Nevertheless, I am still having difficulties in my everyday life.

If possible, please tell me what kind of spiritual disturbance I am under. Also, please teach me what course of life I should take going forward. Thank you very much.

Consecutive Seminars in Kyusyu, "Love, Nurture, and Forgive," held on September 9, 1989, at Munakata YURIX Event Hall in Fukuoka, Japan

---

Life is a workbook of problems to be solved

I have the perfect answer for you: "Life is a workbook of problems to be solved." It is true that you can easily get an answer to your problem by asking me, but it will only solve today's problem. You will face a different problem tomorrow and another one the day after that.

So you do not need to worry about whether you are spiritually disturbed. If you have studied the teachings of Happy Science, then you should already know the cause. You must have heard about the Law of Same Wavelengths' Attraction. I have clearly taught that you and what is possessing you are on the same wavelength. What has possessed you is not the point. What is in your mind has attracted it, so your enemy is not outside you but within you. Spiritual disturbance is not the problem here. What is in your mind invited the evil spirit. So you must discover what that is and discard it. Then, the evil spirit will stop coming.

You do not need to consider getting an exorcism. All you need to do is solve your own problems. OK? Look within yourself and check what you have found against the books of Truth. I have written many books, so you can find what you have done wrong. Unless you discover what you need to correct on your own, you are not really learning. You must fight through it; otherwise, you can never get rid of spiritual disturbances. You are brave enough to ask a question in front of this audience, so you should be able to discover the answer on your own by questioning yourself.

Since you mentioned you have repented about your past, you should already have an idea of the type of mistakes you have committed the most. Unless you face them head-on, you will never be able to defeat them. Remember that the enemy is not outside of you but within. First, find the cause.

Once you know what it is, you can change it. If you cannot take back what you have done in the past, you can only change what you will do in the future.

I have fought a battle similar to yours. Nobody taught me how or what I had to fight. I have an example I can share with you. Over 10 years ago, I had a strong sense of unhappiness. Because of it, I could never say anything nice about other people. I was suffering from an inferiority complex.

One of the characteristics of people who are suffering from an inferiority complex is that they cannot praise others. They can never congratulate others. Whenever they flatter someone, it is always followed by criticism. These kinds of people will surely speak ill of others after praising them.

Once I realized I had this tendency, I knew I had to fight it somehow. It took almost five years for me to feel that I could tame the unruly, wild horse inside of me. It still got unruly from time to time, but I could tighten the reins to keep it under control so that I did not get thrown off. It took me five years to get this far.

That is the reality. It is not an easy task. You cannot correct it in a moment. Just thinking about it for a moment will not fix the problem. So once you identify the fault you want to fix, make a long-term plan over a few years to work on it.

Another point I want to share is mostly for adult men, but it also applies to some women. Nearly 70 percent of worries they have come from their financial situation. This is the truth. Financial circumstance tends to be a blind spot for people who strictly focus on exploring their minds. But many people's sufferings are linked to their financial situations. They might complain about their job performance, promotions, and other things, but it all comes down to their financial instability. It then branches off into trouble at home and other issues.

I am not sure if this applies to you, but if financial matters are one of your concerns, please know that heaven will not lend a helping hand. Money does not fall from the sky. You might have to search through the bamboo grove to find a stash*. [*Audience laughs.*]

Money will not fall from the sky. You only have yourself to rely on. You must develop your own method to increase your financial capacity. There is no other way. If your current job does not pay you enough, you will have to find a way to supplement your income or look for a better-paying job. Either way, be courageous and act. By taking action, most of your worries will be solved.

My answers may not have been what you were expecting, but I spoke in this way because I felt that you were not serious enough about seeking the Truth.

---

* The author is referring to the news where 100 million yen was found in a bamboo grove.

5

Dealing with a Volatile Mother-in-Law

Q5

I am having trouble with my mother-in-law. She is 62 years old and has quite a volatile personality. Although I have no hostile feelings toward her, she sometimes suddenly takes her anger out on me; and when she does, I cannot walk or speak, as if I'm paralyzed. Please give me some advice on what I can do to improve my relationship with her, such as prayers I can recite. My husband is the eldest son of the chief monk of a temple, so his mother was worried about my family background when we got married.

The Second Seminar for Housewives,
held on May 17, 1989, at the Happy Science Training Hall
in Nishi-Ogikubo, Tokyo, Japan

Volatility, spiritual possession, and health are related to each other

You live in a temple. OK, I understand you. It seems you began to realize what has been going on as you were asking the question.

I do feel something spiritual. I can strongly sense the presence of spirits. Now that you mentioned "temple," I am absolutely sure. There is no mistake.

There is a spiritual atmosphere or zone surrounding a temple. To be honest with you, I would not want to live in a graveyard. You might think it would not matter as long as your mind is well-balanced and bright, but a bond is formed when you live near such places. In general, a connection is made when you are physically close. So it is best not to get yourself involved. As long as you live there, stray spirits will be waiting for the opportunity to attack you.

In your mother-in-law's case, I can sense two or three spirits possessing her. Probably three spirits are around her. Indeed, she is possessed by them. I am sure.

The theories taught at Happy Science will help people address issues just like yours. All our teachings can help you understand what you need to do. That is precisely why I have compiled all these books.

The next time you are verbally attacked by your mother-in-law and she aggressively criticizes you, please remind yourself that it is not coming from her. The spirits who possess her are the ones speaking through her. Hopefully, this way of thinking will give you a layer of emotional padding between you and your mother-in-law. Remember, the spirits are yelling through your mother-in-law.

She also needs help. You must help her somehow. Her volatile emotions are troubling her.

In many cases, elderly people's failing health could be the reason why they display their volatile emotions. In truth, they are not the type of people who would do terrible things. They even appear to have relatively clear minds, yet they are emotionally volatile, probably due to spiritual possession. I suspect this is because their health is declining. Either they are suffering from an illness or they get tired easily. For example, their legs, in particular, get weaker as they age.

Therefore, you should help her get better. You can exorcise evil spirits just by helping her improve her health. It is difficult to repel evil spirits when someone is not healthy. This is a critical point.

You can prioritize your mother-in-law's health and help her stay healthy. Think about what you can do for a 62-year-old woman to improve her health. You can pay attention to what she eats and her daily activities. You can also look for other exercises for her and get her involved in activities. I encourage you to bear her health in mind and be creative in what you can do for her to stay healthy. This is the first step.

A healthy person is generally in a good mood. As long as someone is in a good mood, evil spirits cannot easily possess that person. A good mood can repel evil spirits. On the contrary, it is very difficult to exorcise evil spirits when someone is feeling weak and fatigued.

The first thing you can do for her is help improve her health so she can wake up in the morning in a good mood and feel refreshed.

Practical tips for fighting against evil spirits

Another piece of advice I want to give you is to avoid retaliating. When you can tell that multiple evil spirits are verbally abusing you through her, there is no point in responding. Engaging in an argument with them is like taking poison, so let it go. Forget about it. Ignore what she says because it is only temporary and is coming from the spirits who possess her.

Instead, what you can do is wait for her to be in the best mood. Observe your mother-in-law and look for the moment when she is in a very good mood. Show her that you care about her when she is relaxed, such as when she is sitting in the sun and sunbathing. Your caring acts will most likely reach her soul when her state of mind is at peace. Speak to her in your kindest and most considerate tone. Continue to pay attention and be caring to her.

Most evil spirits are full of dissatisfaction and complaints. Consequently, people possessed by evil spirits are also discontent. Nevertheless, even evil spirits can feel kindness. They recognize kindness. So you must try to show kindness with concrete examples.

There is no need to present the greatest act of kindness. Just include small acts of kindness in your everyday life. Your subtle kindness will be enough. Express your sympathy by telling your mother to enjoy her day when she is about to go out. When she returns, offer her a hot cup of tea or ask her if she would like to take a bath first. Something along the lines of these daily exchanges could show her that you are paying attention to her and showering her with kindness.

Evil spirits are the weakest against kindness. You might find it surprising, but there is no need to fight them with power. They become weak when they are treated kindly. They will wither like a slug sprinkled with salt. This is what your "doctor" is prescribing you to treat your problems. So follow the prescription and always speak kindly to your mother-in-law.

Finally, you mentioned that your mother-in-law was apprehensive about her son marrying you. She must still be thinking that you do not fit into the family tradition.

There are two ways to deal with the situation. One is to argue back and tell her to shut up. Another way is to be grateful for being accepted into the family despite her reservations. If possible, I hope you will choose the latter mindset. You will do well if you can manage to stay thankful for the opportunity you were given to be part of the family.

This is going to be a prolonged battle for you. Your mother-in-law will eventually pass away, so it will be a test of your endurance.

However, it might not end with her death. You will have more to think about later if you do not treat her well while she is still alive. Imagine where she would go after she dies. She would not go to anyone but you. You would be struck with lower back pain, paralysis in your legs, rheumatism, asthma, stiff shoulders, constant headaches, and other symptoms. So you should get rid of all possible causes beforehand. Do your best to help her depart from this world with a happy state of mind.

Take this as an opportunity to practice the Truth. If you can help your mother-in-law change herself, you have succeeded. I have already taught many ways to do this, so please be ingenious and apply what you think will work. Of course, reciting "The True Words Spoken By Buddha" and the "Prayers Book" will be very effective. Do not dislike having to deal with your mother-in-law but instead be patient with her and think of her as learning material for you. Anyhow, I taught you where the cause of the problem lies.

6

Studying the Truth to
Exorcise Possessing Spirits

Q6

I heard that when someone I know recommended your lecture CD (cassette tape at the time of this lecture) to two friends, one complained about experiencing numbness and pain in both hands and could not listen to it for long. The other complained about feeling very heavy after listening to it briefly and begged to stop playing it.

What would be the best approach to recommend your teachings to these types of people from now on?

The Seventh Public Lecture of 1990, "The Declaration of Victory," held on July 8, 1990, at Morioka City Ice Arena in Iwate, Japan

---

Why some people suffer
when they listen to my lecture CDs

Some people's hands start shaking when they listen to my lecture CDs because they are possessed. In most cases, they are possessed by snake spirits, and this will show in their hands, feet, or neck.

So the first friend was clearly possessed. People tend to experience spiritual phenomena when they listen to my lectures. Their spiritual channel might not be open, but because they have been possessed for so long, they are extremely sensitive to spiritual matters. You can easily tell by their reactions.

The other friend apparently felt very heavy, so he or she must have been possessed by a few human spirits. When a person under possession listens to my CDs, the spirits possessing them also listen because they are connected. So they all suffer together.

CDs are an especially powerful medium because they contain the original vibrations. So the spirits haunting the person will suffer quite a lot. CDs are about three times as powerful as books.

If the person under possession is heavily influenced by evil spirits, my recordings will cause them to react in one of two ways. They will either become completely free from possession or lose total control of themselves, as if they have become insane.

Therefore, if they react violently to my CDs, you should stop and offer them my books instead. Once my lecture is typed up and printed on paper, the vibration is reduced to about one-third of that contained in a CD. They will still feel the vibration, but it should not result in them acting violently. You can introduce my books to them little by little and help them gradually change their mindset.

By doing this, the thin layers of dark clouds covering their minds will be removed, layer by layer. After that, you can offer them my CDs again, and they will be able to listen without any problems. When the possession weakens, the spirit can be easily removed. That is how things work.

For example, what will happen if a psychiatrist plays my CDs in the psychiatric ward? I do not recommend you try it because I can imagine the chaos it would bring. I can imagine the violent reaction it could cause.

How to cope with long-term possession

Anyhow, what is happening to the two friends is very clear. All you need to do is learn how to deal with their situations. Just as I have explained, the friends are possessed. This is a fact. You should be able to identify their problem by talking to them. The issue lies within their own mind. You will need to teach them what it is or perhaps recommend my books that will teach them how to correct their mind. You need to find the right book for them.

Persistence is key. Those two friends did not suddenly come under heavy possession. It took them a few years or possibly 10 or 20 years to form dark clouds in their mind, which the spirits possessing them were attracted to. Some evil spirits who possess people for years may believe that they are serving as guardian spirits. In that case, it will be very difficult to get rid of the possession.

There is something called the law of inertia. A speeding train will not stop immediately after applying the brakes. A bicycle will not stop right away, either. The same applies to cars and people who are running. If you suddenly try to stop, the train could derail, or the car could tip over.

Similarly, the total amount of negative energy accumulated through your thoughts and actions will not be canceled out unless you accumulate an equal amount of positive energy. If you attempt to instantly wipe out large debts by applying an extremely strong light of Truth, the consequence could be overwhelming. It is best to spend some time getting familiar with the Truth.

This type of reaction occurs not only with CDs but also at my lecture events. I suspect some of you in the audience have experienced it. Some people are too scared to enter the venue. They will stop at the gate, or they cannot enter through the door. Even if they made it to their seats and sat through my lecture, as soon as they leave, they return to the dreadful condition they were in before they came.

Nevertheless, the reason is clear, as I explained earlier. I cannot treat every single person because I am not a doctor working in an emergency room, so please fight on your own based on the things I have explained.

Be persistent—that is the key. The friends are under evil spiritual influences, but those spirits are outsiders. The real owner of the physical body is the soul that resides inside. The soul and the body are connected by the Silver Cord, and they are an exact match for each other. Therefore, it is incredibly difficult for another spirit to completely take over the body.

Even if you are possessed by a spirit, you, too are a spirit. You have more power over your body, so you are much stronger than the possessing spirit. As long as you can get a hold of yourself, you will never lose. So believe in yourself, study the Truth, and push back on the evil spirit little by little. That is the way to do it.

The effective power of a transparent mind

Here are some examples of the proof that the evil spirits have left you. If you feel something warm come into your heart when you hear my lecture, listen to my CDs, or read my books, then it means God's Light is flowing into you. You are no longer possessed. The spirits possessing you have left your body.

While these spirits possess you, they can be quite a nuisance. But when the Light enters your body and expels the possessing spirits, your body will feel much lighter. Please remember that. You will be surprised at how much lighter your shoulders feel. If you experience this wonderful feeling, it means you have repelled the evil spirits on your own by making advancements in your study of the Truth, so look forward to it.

Many company workers are in poor physical condition every single day. They are chronically fatigued and cannot think straight anymore. Of course, this could be due to alcohol. But even those kinds of people can study the Truth and make their minds transparent. As they learn the Truth, a time will come when they feel something peel off of them. That is when they will feel much lighter, mentally and physically. It is when evil spirits are stripped away.

Once the evil spirits are removed, they will have a hard time taking back their control over the living person's body. It is very important not to miss this opportunity to completely cut ties with them. Seize the moment and change the direction of your mind by studying the Truth.

When you do, your mind will firmly point in a direction that is different from that of the evil spirits. You might still have a bad day once in a while, but eventually, they will be less and less likely to interfere with you. Evil spirits will realize that you are now out of their reach. That is what you will experience.

Anyhow, although those friends are possessed, they are good examples to prove the efficacy of the Truth. Someone who is under much more serious possession will fall into a deep sleep after hearing my CD for just a few minutes. Evil spirits will prevent them from listening to the CD by putting them to sleep. This is a typical sign, so if you have fallen asleep during my lecture, please reflect deeply on yourself. If you dozed off during the lecture today, I suggest you think carefully about why and try to deal with it.

That is my answer. Please be patient. Do not rush the process. Be slow and steady. That is the best way.

CHAPTER THREE

How to Overcome
Spiritual Sensitivity

1

Avoiding and Shutting Off Negative Vibrations

Q1

Now, as I study the Truth, I am more sensitive to God's light. However, at the same time, my heart starts to pound when I am near an angry person. When we study the Truth, does it make us more sensitive to negative vibrations? If so, how can we overcome this?

The Third Special Lecture of 1990, "The Surging Great River of Love,"
held on November 23, 1990, at Okinawa Convention Center in Okinawa, Japan

Having the ability to tell the difference is a blessing

I believe you cannot simply say that being more susceptible to God's Light is good and being more vulnerable to the vibrations of evil spirits is bad. It is a little too simple-minded to think in such a dualistic, good-or-bad way.

Let me explain this using music as an example. If you study music, you develop a better understanding of it. If you like classical music and listen to it often, you can judge the caliber of the conductor and the performances of the violin and the piano at a concert better than an average person who has never studied music. The more you study, the more you will know.

Naturally, the more you study music, the harder it becomes for you to listen to terrible performances. You become more sensitive and notice various things, such as the conductor being a little off-beat or the pianist showing off a little. Consequently, you will become more selective about the music you can enjoy.

Suppose you are at a classical concert, which you find hard to listen to, and look at the people around you. You will notice that many of them are joyfully applauding the music, which makes you wonder, "Does being ignorant bring greater joy?" People who are amateurs in music can enjoy, applaud, and shout "Bravo!" to any musical performance. On the other hand, people who know more about music will find it difficult to enjoy every concert. As you learn more about music, you will be able to tell when a performance is mediocre.

But does this mean people who know nothing about music are better off and happier? I do not think so. To be able to tell that something is actually bad is a blessing. You will be happier knowing that an orchestra is performing poorly than staying blind to it. That is because being able to tell whether something is good or bad will also allow you to easily tell when a performance is superb and of high quality. The joy you feel in such moments is truly of a spiritual nature.

Similarly, studying the Truth will make you more sensitive to evil vibrations. You will quickly sense whether someone's level of enlightenment is low or where they are wrong. But it is the same as the example of music I mentioned above.

The same goes for other fields of art. If you have studied art, you will not be able to stand terrible paintings. But amateurs in art will find any painting great. Likewise, those with a poor sense of taste will say every dish is delicious, but when they acquire a better palate, they will be able to distinguish between different flavors.

Now, who do you think is happier, those who can tell whether something tastes bad or those who think everything they eat tastes great? Perhaps it is unclear who is happier when seen from a general perspective. But I have to say that knowing more brings you more happiness. Being able to tell the difference is something to be happy about. I believe this type of happiness is advanced and sophisticated.

You say you are troubled because the more you study the Truth, the more you can sense and feel the presence of evil spirits, but I have to say: that is a high-class problem. Other people cannot tell the difference even if they want to, so you should be happy that you have such an ability.

When you make further progress in studying the Truth, you will no longer go to "poor-quality classical concerts" and instead choose "truly impressive classical concerts." This means that as you raise your level of enlightenment, you will accordingly interact with people who have the same level of awareness. This will also lead you to more important work. So there will always be a higher level of joy in store for you.

2

What to Keep in Mind after Opening Your Spiritual Window

Q2

I would like to ask you about the spiritual channel and the strict life that awaits us after opening it. Also, I would like to know whether those who are ahead in studying the Truth, such as Happy Science lecturers, have opened their spiritual channel.

The Ninth Public Lecture of 1990, "The Enlightenment of the Great Universe," held on August 26, 1990, at Makuhari Messe in Chiba, Japan

---

Two types of spiritually sensitive people

Regarding your first question about what will become of you when you open your spiritual channel, the teachings of Happy Science have all the answers.

We do not use "surgical methods" to deal with an open spiritual channel but encourage the "internal medicine approach"—in other words, we write "prescriptions" that do not damage people's souls.

For example, when a person opens their spiritual channel and undergoes dangerous spiritual phenomena, we could use a surgical method, but doing so would significantly change their life. It is risky, like making a bet; it could either be a success or a failure. Therefore, we use the internal medicine approach. I would like you to study the Truth and awaken on your own. If you make mistakes, I want you to be able to correct yourself and return to the right path. This is not a quick method, but it is indeed the Royal Road.

If you open your spiritual channel by chance, you will hear the voices of various spirits and see them; they may also enter your body and speak all kinds of things through your mouth. You may find this phenomenon entertaining at first, but you will gradually lose control of yourself and be possessed 24/7.

The spirits may sound wise in the beginning, but they will eventually say something odd. By the time you realize that you must do something about it, you will no longer be able to control yourself. It would be OK if you could control yourself like you would a puppet on a string, but by that stage, you will be manipulated by the possessing spirits instead, as if you are being pulled by a piano wire. You will no longer be yourself. This is how opening your spiritual channel too early can end in tragedy.

However, those who are talented or have good potential in developing their spiritual ability only need a small trigger to open their spiritual channel. Many of them can open it by simply listening to my lectures, attending Happy Science seminars, or reading my books.

Here is my advice for those kinds of people. Being spiritually sensitive is a relatively common trait. These people can quickly connect with the spiritual world, but that does not necessarily mean their souls are superior to others.

There are two types of people who are quick to open their spiritual channel. One is those who underwent spiritual discipline in their past lives. These people awaken to their spiritual ability quite early on, but they might not have done spiritual training in the right way in their past lives. There are all kinds of training. Let's say they focused too much on attaining supernatural powers in their past lives. In that case, it will be easier for them to open their spiritual channel during this lifetime because their spiritual trigger lies in the shallow part of their soul.

The second type is those who are subject to severe spiritual disturbances. They will experience something similar to opening their spiritual channel. These people are constantly possessed by five or more evil spirits. They are under the complete control of the spirits and have lost their sense of self.

First, learn to control your mind in the right way

Some people may have relatives or family members who are spiritually sensitive. Others may have grown up in a family environment where many lost spirits were present for certain reasons. Those people are vulnerable and easily influenced by spirits. Also, lots of people have become spiritually sensitive after joining different kinds of religious groups.

Whatever your situation is, you must first remember to control your mind in the right way. To teach what is right from various perspectives, I have been publishing all sorts of spiritual messages and theoretical books of Truth. You will gain a better understanding as you keep reading my books. Those who are spiritually sensitive will realize that by exploring Right Mind, which I teach in my books, they will gain peace of mind, and their body will feel light and warm.

On the contrary, if you are doing the opposite of what I teach, your body will always feel heavy, and you will not have peace of mind. Many thoughts will be continuously running through your head. Also, you will be easily triggered by other people's words. You will have a short temper, and you will not lend an ear to other people's opinions. This is a typical sign that evil spirits are influencing you. When evil spirits influence you, you often become less flexible, reject other people's opinions, have a bad temper, and become self-centered. These are the characteristics of a person under the influence of evil spirits.

If you study the teachings of Happy Science, you will see that they teach you to be the opposite of those traits. For example, I teach you to live your life for the sake of others as well as the methods to keep your mind at peace. As you practice the teachings, you will learn to take control of your mind. You will be able to sense when an evil spirit is nearby, and you will know what to do. As you continue to steer your mind correctly, evil spirits will naturally leave you and will not be able to possess you. That is when you will emit a halo. When you emit light, evil spirits cannot possess you.

If you become extremely spiritually sensitive, it usually takes about a year to control your mind and completely shut out evil spirits. You will need to put in that much effort. What is important is that you shut out spiritual influences using your own will. No matter how hard the spirits try to talk to you, regardless of what they say to you and the effect they have on you, you must shut them out using your own will. It is crucial that you strengthen your will to shut out evil spirits.

As for our lecturers and whether they have opened their spiritual channel, some of them do have it open. Even if they do not, they should be spiritually sensitive enough to tell if someone is possessed or not. They may not be able to tell whether you are guided by high spirits [*laughs jokingly*], but they will know whether evil spirits possess you. So you can assume they can make a faithful judgment. Let's say one of our members claims to have opened their spiritual channel. Our lecturers will definitely be able to tell whether what that person says and writes is genuine.

To become a member of Happy Science, you must submit an application with an essay (at the time this lecture was held), and if you are under severe spiritual disturbance, you will be rejected. Unfortunately, if you are spiritually disturbed, you cannot become a member. This is one of the reasons we started this application system.

I, myself, no longer judge the essays. Our lecturers are doing this task now. Most of them will know whether an applicant is under spiritual disturbance by reading his or her essay; they will not be able to read a possessed person's essay through to the end. Lecturers gradually become more spiritual, and they develop the ability to recognize evil spirits.

At Happy Science, I do not encourage our lecturers to conduct spiritual phenomena such as spiritual channeling very often because it will most likely drive them mad. For example, suppose you are a non-member who is influenced by evil spirits. The evil spirits influencing you will probably not be devils. But if you are a lecturer of Happy Science, powerful devils will come and attack you, which will be very tough for you to deal with. Evil spirits that accord with the level of your soul will come to you.

That is why I tell our lecturers to base their work on the laws and theories of Happy Science and not on their spiritual abilities or powers.

3

Become One with the Supporting Spirit Group of Happy Science to Defeat Evil Spirits

Q3

I believe we will become more spiritually sensitive as we deepen our practice of self-reflection. And I'm sure we will encounter people with different faith as we spread our teachings. Can you please advise us on how to be resilient against their spiritual vibration?

The Third Special Seminar of 1990,
"A Lecture on Self-Reflection Methods (Self-Reflection as Buddha's Disciples),"
held on October 14, 1990, at Shizuoka Industrial Hall in Shizuoka, Japan

How to gain support from the supporting spirit group of Happy Science

OK. Of course, you might have to fight against evil vibrations or spirits by yourself sometimes, but what I also want you to think about is the time you are living in now. The Happy Science movement has begun and is making progress as we speak. This is made possible by the support of the supporting spirit group. Once I leave this world, things may change; but until then, you will not be defeated as long as you are firmly connected to me and the Happy Science supporting spirits through faith. Although people from other religious organizations may come at you with evil vibrations, you must be determined to stay connected to us through faith.

While I am alive on earth, Happy Science is directly connected to the supporting spirit group. As long as you have a firm grip on this rope of faith, you will never lose against evil spirits. There may be times when you have to fight against evil spirits that you cannot deal with by yourself, but as long as you hold on to this rope of faith, evil spirits will have to fight against the supporting spirit group of Happy Science. This is what faith means. Simply put, having faith means you are connected to the original source.

No evil spirit can fight against a supporting spirit group of 500 spirits. In contrast, it is easy for evil spirits to go after and take down someone who has let go of this rope of faith. So tell yourself, "I won't lose because I have the Happy Science supporting spirit group with me and because Master himself is alive on earth and leading us. I will never lose. I can do this. I will win." If you believe this and make the necessary effort, you will win. If you think you will lose, then you will. So please stay strong. That is what it means to have faith.

Staying connected through faith means you are spiritually connected to the entire supporting spirit group. Therefore, you are not fighting alone; instead, the supporting spirit group will fight in your place. If they do not fight for you, it means there is something wrong with your faith. Please think this way.

4

Repelling Negative Vibrations

Q4

One of my relatives who belongs to another religious organization asked me whether Happy Science can repel vibrations. He says that his teacher can do it. His teacher tells him, "Develop a body that can sense spiritual vibrations. Train your mind so that you are not influenced by those vibrations and repel them." How can I explain the teachings of Happy Science regarding this to him?

The Second Thursday Seminar, "A Lecture on Chapter Two of *The Laws of the Sun*," held on October 20, 1988, at Happy Science Training Hall in Nishi-Ogikubo, Tokyo

Safety measures against negative spiritual vibrations: avoid making connections

Spiritual vibrations are as real as they can be. I am surrounded by spiritual vibrations daily. I publish all kinds of books month after month, but being involved in creative work, like being an author, is not compatible with worldly vibrations in the first place. My productivity in creative work drops when

I have to take care of office work and meet with different people. This is because I am subjected to the vibrations of the people I meet. Each person has their own vibration. They often carry worldly vibrations. As I spend time with them, my vibrations begin to match theirs so that I can talk on their level. It cannot be helped. Then, I will be under the influence of their vibrations for a while.

In this way, even if I am in a meditative state, it may be disturbed depending on the person I meet and the type of work I must do. My vibrations will stay uninterrupted if I do not meet anyone. But when I interact with various types of people and do various kinds of work, my meditative state gets disrupted.

I assume the vibrations your relative is referring to are spiritual vibrations. I think what he means is how you repel the spiritual vibrations of people's negative thought energy and the thought energy of lower-level spirits when you encounter them. This is extremely difficult, partly because there is no end to getting rid of spiritual vibrations like this.

Nevertheless, I have two pieces of advice for you. The first one is, "Do not make connections with negative spiritual vibrations." This is the best way. There is no better way than to avoid making connections with negative thoughts and vibrations from evil spirits. Of course, there are many ways to repel evil vibrations, but please do not make ties with them in the first place. This is truly the best option.

Especially when you become spiritually sensitive, you will be affected by spiritual vibrations much more easily. So please avoid connecting with people who are possessed by evil spirits or going to religious organizations that are full of evil spirits; there is no end to repelling them. You are better off avoiding those people or groups, if possible.

Of course, some people may take on the challenge of changing evil vibrations into good vibrations, which is OK. But for most of you, in general, I suggest that you avoid getting affected by evil vibrations.

Using myself as an example, I felt much more at ease once I renounced my secular life. It was tough working at a company. The phones were ringing, and people were always talking very loudly. I obviously could not concentrate my mind because I would look spaced out if I did and because it was impossible not to receive worldly vibrations. So the reality was that it was tough to work there. Because you cannot completely avoid being subjected to spiritual vibrations, the best way to keep yourself safe is by proactively not making any ties or connections to them.

Using self-power measures
against evil spirits: self-reflection

My second piece of advice is about the measures you can take against evil spirits. I will teach you properly about how to exorcise and deal with evil spirits at some point (Note); basically, there are two ways: by self-power and by outside power.

The first thing you must do using self-power is self-reflection. Many of you may think of self-reflection as a moral act, but if you are spiritually sensitive or have opened your spiritual channel, you will know that it is much more than a moral act.

For example, let's say I am possessed by an evil spirit, and I practice self-reflection. I would start by looking back at what I did and thought in the morning. Perhaps I was sleepy when I woke up or I wanted to skip going to the Secretariat Division. As I continue to reflect on myself, the evil spirit possessing me begins to shake or shiver. Then, as I reflect on myself deeper and become more skilled at it, the evil spirit will no longer be able to possess me. I will feel as if something has peeled off from me.

Of course, not everyone will realize this, but I must say many of you in the audience also carry "regular customers." As you reflect deeper on yourself, you will feel something peel off from you. You do not need to open your spiritual channel to feel this. Your body will actually feel lighter.

How are you all feeling so far? Are you tired? You will become very weary if you have "regulars" with you. It won't bother you so much once you get used to it, but your body will always feel heavy, as if you are wearing heavy clothes. You will be tired and drowsy.

But if you practice self-reflection, you will eventually reach a point where your body feels lighter. After you reflect on yourself enough, you will feel lighter. You will feel as if something has peeled off from you. Your body will suddenly feel much lighter. You will be surprised to know how light it feels to live in this world and how light your body is.

This is self-reflection or one way to deal with evil spirits using self-power.

Alternatives to self-reflection: humility and gratitude

Of course, there are other measures you can take using self-power. For example, you can learn to be humble. This is similar to the practice of self-reflection. People who are captivated by evil spirits are often arrogant and extremely proud of themselves.

Generally, those who are full of pride, egoistic, or cannot stand having their pride being hurt even the slightest cannot reflect on themselves. That is because they cannot humble themselves or admit that they were wrong. Hence, they guard themselves with their pride, which means they cannot self-reflect. The only way these people can deal with evil spirits is by learning to be humble. To become humble, they must first lower their self-image. They must look at themselves with a clean slate.

Proud people think they are entitled to special treatment. They have high expectations of themselves, so they think it is natural for them to be treated above a certain level. Their self-evaluation is too high, and they cannot lower it. These people cannot self-reflect. If this is the case, they must lower their self-image. I hope you can understand what I'm saying.

Suppose you are quite talented but feel mistreated at work. You think everyone other than you is an idiot and less competent than you. So you cannot accept the fact that you are in the same section as them. Usually, these kinds of people cannot reflect on themselves. I recommend that they lower their self-evaluation and see things from that viewpoint. They can start by learning to control their thoughts. This is similar to the practice of "it's enough" mind. You must see yourself from a clean slate.

For instance, if you feel mistreated at work despite graduating from a good school, put aside your educational background. Let's say you are 22 years old, and you started working at a company after graduating from university. You work with many kinds of people there, and among them is a coworker who graduated from a community college and started working a year before you. Although this person is younger than you, he or she is most likely more capable at work than you. I notice many women struggle with something like this. What are they struggling with? It is their pride. The coworker is younger than them, yet they can do a better job. This is where people create inner conflicts. They panic.

If you are feeling this way, you should first put aside things like your age and education. Look at yourself simply as who you are now, and think about what you are capable of. You may then realize that you can only serve coffee to your coworkers. Just take things easy and start from the bottom. So first, you should lower your self-image. This is another way.

Those who are possessed by evil spirits truly despise the idea of lowering themselves. Listen carefully. Put your hands on your chest and think honestly. People who are possessed by evil spirits hate to lower their self-esteem. Do you understand me? They hate to have their reputations ruined or their value lowered. Please consider whether this applies to you.

Start by being humble. If you cannot self-reflect, learn to be humble. Step down from where you are standing. This is the second way.

Another way is to have gratitude—to be thankful. You may not be able to self-reflect, but you can be thankful. Some of you may find it hard to reflect and cannot think of anything, but you can surely be grateful. At the least, you can start by thanking the people who took care of you the most, such as your mother, father, friends, or teachers. It may be tough for you to reflect on yourself, but you can be thankful to those people. Therefore, start by giving thanks to the people who took care of you. Give gratitude to them every night. You can also give gratitude to your guardian spirit. Practicing these things will expel evil spirits and cut off negative vibrations.

Please remember that self-reflection, being humble, and gratitude are things you can do using your own effort.

Measures against evil spirits
using outside power: prayer

You can also exorcise evil spirits with outside power— through prayer. For example, take the *Spiritual Messages from Jesus Christ* (now published internally as *Ryuho Okawa Collection of Spiritual Messages, Vol. 5*, available only in Japanese). This book contains many prayers, and when you read them out loud, you will indeed receive light from heaven. The light comes down.

I am not sure if you can receive the direct light of Jesus Christ, but I can. So spirits who belong to Jesus Christ's group will come down to support you when you recite those prayers. This is one way to receive light through outside power.

Another definite way to deal with evil spirits using outside power is to have high spirits enter your body, although you must have your spiritual channel open to do this. This is the most convenient and quickest way, and I regularly use it. Let's say someone is possessed by evil spirits. As I encounter him or her, I think, "Oh, here it comes." But telling those evil spirits to reflect on themselves or persuading them every time would be an endless task. In these cases, as I do not have time to spend talking to evil spirits, I call a high spirit and have it enter my body. Then, the evil spirits possessing the person will leave at once. That will be all. You can shut out negative vibrations by having a high spirit or your guardian spirit or guiding spirit enter your body. This is also a measure you can take.

What to do when you are attacked by Satan

Please note that a high spirit cannot enter your body when you are under powerful possession, especially if you are intentionally being attacked or tempted not just by any evil spirit but by something like Satan. In that case, high spirits won't come to you no matter how many times you call for them. If that is the case, of course, you must practice self-reflection, have gratitude, pray, and be humble. If you cannot expel evil spirits despite taking those measures, it means you have been attacked by the strongest, most powerful kind of negative vibration.

So what can you do when the likes of Satan target you? As I have mentioned before, it all comes down to how much you can endure. It is like fighting a war of attrition; it is a test of endurance. It is a matter of whether you will become mentally unstable.

Simply put, Satans are either trying to confuse you or drag you down. For example, their intention could be to lead you astray from believing in a certain religion. If you belong to a religious group that is inhabited by many evil spirits, those "guardian" and "guiding" spirits will not want you to join Happy Science. In general, they won't like that.

That is because when you come to Happy Science, your light will grow stronger. Some people feel sick just by trying to visit our training facilities. They suddenly feel unwell, and their legs do not move just because they get on the train to head to Happy Science. These people are undoubtedly possessed. Evil spirits do not want to come to Happy Science. They are afraid of being found out and exorcised, which is why people under possession feel ill. Some people feel unwell just by coming close to Happy Science locations.

I have also heard about people who get stuck in one area and keep going around in circles in the same place. They cannot move on. They may manage to get to the station but have a change of heart and decide to go home; then they change their minds again. They keep going back and forth on repeat. This is a classic example of possession. If you keep going back and forth, unsure whether to come to one of my lectures or not, you are most likely possessed. You are being held back.

Those people think in circles. At first, they are ready to attend my lecture, but the next moment, they feel they must go home and spend time with their family. But then, they want to come to my lecture. They keep going around in circles. These people are proactively attacked by evil spirits. Unfortunately, those evil spirits are hard to remove using the means I mentioned earlier. Then, what should you do? You will have to fight a long-term battle.

The biggest weakness of hellish spirits is that they are impatient. They cannot withstand long battles. They have a short temper; they want instant results. They are not the type to enjoy slow and steady attacks. They like speed and power and like to get things done quickly.

Therefore, if you are being influenced by hellish spirits, tell yourself, "OK, let's take things slow. They are here. I'll make a 10-year plan to get rid of them." You should plan the small acts of discipline you will take over a long period, which is what evil spirits are afraid of the most. This is what they hate the most. They cannot stand seeing you study every day and making your mind brighter. Hellish spirits despise that the most, so let it be your last resort.

You must think of the long run and make gradual progress. If you do that, no evil spirit will be able to keep possessing you. No devil can possess someone who is always making efforts to improve themselves. It is impossible for them. Devils may be able to put you into turmoil for a few days or maybe a week or two. However, as long as you aspire to make improvements and make an effort to climb up the stairs of light little by little, even Satan cannot defeat you.

Hellish spirits are not very energetic. They are not very slow-paced or easygoing. They want to fight a short battle, so they want to bring chaos and destruction to someone's life quickly. So the best countermeasure to this is to draw out the time period. During this time, check to see that you have made improvements, however small they may be.

These are the various means you can take to cut off negative vibrations. I have practiced them all. The last resort is to endure and fight a long battle. If you are being spiritually bothered or intruded upon by evil spirits, maybe it has something to do with your past connection to another religious group.

At another time, I will teach you in more detail about how to block vibrations from evil spirits, but for now, I have taught you the basics.

Why some weird religions can sometimes cure illnesses

I would like to add one more thing. If you are possessed by evil spirits, you cannot expel evil vibrations. Some religious groups teach that you can, but if you are possessed, there is no way you can expel evil vibrations.

If you manage to shut off evil vibrations despite being possessed, it means that an even more powerful evil spirit entered you and scared away the weaker evil spirit that was possessing you. A weaker evil spirit will run away when a stronger one comes, so you can expel evil spirits in that sense. But what is happening is that a stronger evil spirit has replaced a weaker evil spirit. If an even more powerful evil being comes to you, sometimes your illness may be cured. This can occur in weird religions.

For example, let's say that your leg is possessed by an evil spirit, and you go to a weird religion. An even more powerful evil spirit could possess you, and your leg may heal. When an evil spirit encounters something more powerful than itself, it gets scared and runs away; then you will be able to move your leg. This kind of thing really happens. But I wouldn't say that is a method to repel evil vibrations. I hope this answers your question.

(Note) "The Lecture on *How to Exorcise Evil Spirits*" and "The Lecture on *How to Protect Yourself from Evil Spirits*" were held in February 1990 as seminars to screen the candidates for Happy Science lecturers. Both lectures are included in *Faith and Passion*.

5

Guidance for Spiritually Sensitive People

Q5

Ever since I started reading your books, I began channeling various spirits. When I am talking to someone, evil spirits possessing that person tend to attack me aggressively. Please give me advice on how I should handle these spiritual phenomena.

Consecutive Seminars in Kyushu, "Love, Nurture, and Forgive," held on September 9, 1989, at Munakata YURIX Event Hall in Fukuoka, Japan

Be aware and know your limit

It appears that spiritual channeling is a usual occurrence for you. I have no intention of entirely denying what you said. I'm sure more and more members of Happy Science will experience similar situations from now on. In fact, it is already happening to many of our members. The truth is, it is not too difficult to "open the window of your mind." And as Happy Science grows into a larger organization, numerous members will be able to do that.

However, you must keep in mind that humans are not very strong alone. As long as we have a physical body, our abilities will also depend on our physical condition. This is true for both you and me. We are all in the same situation.

I want you to be especially mindful of knowing your limit. I understand you want to make others happy using your spiritual ability, but you must know that you have your limit. In this world, there are countless people who are lost and suffering. Even so, I cannot meet and lead them all to heaven. I myself struggle daily thinking about these things.

Therefore, we must utilize our wisdom as much as possible. If you try to save people with your spiritual abilities by simply exorcising the evil spirits possessing them, you will quickly reach your physical limit. And when you run out of energy, evil spirits will be able to control you instead. Eventually, you will lose; you cannot win that way.

Human beings are indeed like batteries. We cannot release more energy than we charge. If we try to go beyond this limit and release more, we will wear ourselves out. Thus, to recharge yourself, you must study the Truth, of course, but you must rest and eat food as well.

You also need to know exactly how much "electricity" your battery can provide. You might be sad to find out your limit, but you must accept reality. Based on your capacity, you should think about the most efficient way to help each person get better. If the person needs more time to purify their mind, then you can start by giving them hints or opportunities. Or you may come across someone who is simply too much for you to handle. They could be possessed by five, six, or even ten evil spirits and may show no signs of reflecting on themselves. Sometimes you will come across people you can do nothing to help.

These are the most painful times; nevertheless, there is one thing you can do: it is to believe and pray that the person will definitely walk toward God's light when the right time comes. This may be the only thing you can do. Everyone has their own timing. You must believe that their time will come and that things will definitely turn out for the better.

At any rate, you should not be stubborn and think that you can continually fight and expel evil spirits. I myself take precautions and barely use this approach. Humans, indeed, have a limit to how long they can continue exorcising evil spirits on their own. A single human being can only fight off so many evil spirits. He or she will only last for so long.

For example, if you had to perform an exorcism for five or ten people every day, you won't last very long. I know my own limits, so in my case, publishing the teachings and spreading the Truth through my books will have a greater impact. Having more than a thousand people hear me at a lecture event will lead to better results. Releasing the CDs and DVDs of my lectures will also be better.

In this way, I choose to use my time efficiently to maximize the effect of my work. I wish I could give private consultations to Happy Science members and non-members who ask for them, but unfortunately, there are too many of those people. It is far more effective and easier to publish, for example, these Q&A sessions instead. I am always making efforts in this way.

See through to the core problem

I won't question the authenticity of the spiritual phenomena you are experiencing. I acknowledge that you had valuable experiences. Now, I advise you to work on your overall skills and use them to guide others. Please do not let spiritual phenomena control you.

You can guide people with a single phrase. Identify the core problem of the person who is struggling. Find out what lies at the root of their suffering. When you point that out for them, their problems will automatically dissolve.

People who are suffering and under the influence of evil spirits do not know what is at the root of their mistaken thoughts. If they knew their core problem, they wouldn't be influenced by evil spirits in the first place. Unfortunately, they have no idea what is at the root of their problem. That is why you should identify and point out the cause of their problems. You can start by helping them realize it.

I may not have given you the answers you were hoping for, but I hope you will learn that there is a limit to your ability. Please use your wisdom and think about ways to guide many people correctly.

One way is to point out the root of people's problems; this action alone will give them a chance to realize. Then, they will figure out the rest by themselves. Just doing that will be enough to help them.

To be able to see through to the root cause of others' problems, you must go through many experiences and gain insight, be cultured, and have other general overall skills. Therefore, there is no end to studying. You must know this.

Please do not try to solve problems with spiritual abilities alone. This applies to me, too, so please keep this in mind.

6

Sleep and Possession

Q6

I often feel sleepy even though I don't feel physically tired. Please teach us how to fight off drowsiness.

The Third Public Lecture of 1988, "The Principle of Salvation," held on July 31, 1988, at Edogawa-Ku Cultural Center in Tokyo, Japan

Spiritually sensitive people need to sleep longer

I will answer your question based on two aspects.

The first aspect is that sleep is vital for spiritually sensitive people. This is because spiritually sensitive people get easily exhausted compared with ordinary people who are less spiritually sensitive. They get mentally exhausted.

People who only use their surface consciousness are fond of living within worldly vibrations and can live without many problems. On the other hand, those who have a crack in their surface consciousness—in other words, those who have access to their subconscious—are easily exhausted when they encounter worldly vibrations. This actually happens to them.

People who tend to become exhausted from worldly vibrations require more sleep. I have already mentioned in my books that when people sleep, their souls often leave their bodies. This is called astral projection. It happens a few times in one night. When you are dreaming, your soul is often away from your body.

Your soul leaves your body because it needs to absorb energy from the Real World; it leaves to recharge through receiving spiritual energy from the Spiritual Sun. Your body feels re-energized after sleep because you not only rested your physical body but also recharged yourself with spiritual energy. That is why spiritually sensitive people require long hours of sleep and why they become sleepy during the day.

From what I can tell, you seem very spiritually sensitive. That may be why you get sleepy. Please get some sleep if you have time. You should sleep at 8 p.m., or even earlier, at 7 p.m., if you can. If you are a housewife and can take a nap during the day, then you should. It is good to take a nap because it will prevent evil spirits from coming to you. You can build spiritual resistance against evil spirits by increasing your sleeping hours. Try to finish your work early and sleep longer, even if it is by an hour. This should prevent you from getting sleepy during the day. I believe it is because you are spiritually sensitive. This is the first aspect.

Why you may be getting sleepy
while studying the Truth

Now, I will move on to the second aspect. I think some of you in the audience felt sleepy during my lecture today. I am not talking about those who fell asleep because they thought my lecture was boring. Some people are always dozy during my lecture. Others cannot remember what I said in the lecture; it goes in one ear and out the other. And some feel as if they have headphones on; they hear my words but cannot grasp what I mean. These people definitely have something over their heads. All three types of people are being obstructed spiritually. They will drift off to sleep, even when they listen to the CDs or watch the DVDs of my lecture.

This is because whatever is possessing these people is preventing them from listening to my teachings. If they listen to my lectures, they may possibly experience a spiritual awakening. If so, evil spirits will no longer be able to possess them, meaning those spirits will lose their "home." Evil spirits will lose the "home" they have finally found. It is difficult for evil spirits to find a new home to settle into nowadays. Even if they go out searching for one, most people are already possessed by other evil spirits.

Do you know how *ayu* or sweetfish protect their territory? When they find another fish near their feeding territory, they come racing back to protect it. Evil spirits act similarly. They do not like to share their territories or be with other evil spirits. They have likes and dislikes and do not want to possess someone who is already possessed by others. They want to find a new home that is theirs and enjoy possessing that person. So they prefer to possess someone who is not yet possessed.

Evil spirits do not want to lose the habitat they have worked so hard to get. They want to keep people under their possession, but sadly for them, some of those people want to attend my lecture. Evil spirits will be in trouble if the people they have possessed awaken spiritually. That is why they cover those people's ears to block out what I say.

In this case, evil spirits are causing their drowsiness. As soon as the conversation turns to the topic of the Truth, they suddenly become drowsy. I myself have witnessed this before. I once played my lecture CDs to a person under spiritual possession, and as soon I did, he fell fast asleep. He went entirely unconscious. This was a case of heavy possession. He was possessed by more than four or five evil spirits. He fell into a deep sleep. If you see people who seem to have "headphones" on, you can assume they are possessed by more than four or five evil spirits.

7

Prescriptions for Spiritually Sensitive People

Q7

In today's lecture, you mentioned the story of how Jesus felt his energy being drained from him when a woman touched the hem of his robe. I think that I'm spiritually sensitive, too. When I talk to people or interact with many people at work, I feel physically drained.

I have reflected on myself many times, yet I cannot find a solid solution to this issue. So I would appreciate it if you could teach me how to stop my energy from being drained, keep the needle of my mind pointed in a positive direction, and not be discouraged by fatigue.

The Second Special Seminar of 1990,
"A Lecture on the Methods of Meditation—Meditation of the Great Ocean,"
held on July 22, 1990, at Takatsuki City Hall in Osaka, Japan

Plan your daily or weekly routine

That is a high-class problem. I wish someone would teach *me* instead [*laughs*]. I also get quite tired, so I wish someone would tell me how to overcome it. Anyhow, some people get very tired when they go to crowded places. These people are spiritually sensitive to a certain level. On the other hand, some people become energetic and excited when they are in a crowd. They are a different type of people. They are most likely emitting the same kind of energy as the crowd. I also get tired when I go to crowded places and become exhausted after meeting many people. It is because I am spiritually sensitive, and so are you.

If you are spiritually sensitive, you must maintain your daily routine. The most important thing for you is to not wreck your lifestyle. Various things happen in our lives, and sometimes we can be shaken up by them. That is why you must maintain your daily lifestyle. You should create your own pattern, your daily routine. You should find a basic lifestyle pattern that is the best fit for you. I understand you have to interact with many people, but it is crucial that you maintain this basic routine.

Of course, it is good to be sociable, but you should make your boundaries clear. You should let others know what type of person you are. We, humans, cannot read each other's minds, so we do various things without being considerate of each other. Therefore, if you set your own rules and tell others what you think and want to do, they will engage with you accordingly. They will engage and interact with you without crossing your boundaries. Letting others know your boundaries will help you significantly.

Sleep is most important for those who get tired easily; it is essential for them. Usually, spiritually sensitive people especially require longer sleeping hours than people who are not spiritually sensitive. Their standard sleeping hours are a little longer than average. Cutting down even one or two hours of sleep will significantly affect them. So if you usually sleep for eight hours but cut your sleep by an hour or two, meaning you sleep for six or seven hours, you will feel out of energy from midday onward. Cutting your hours of sleep will affect you severely.

Of course, we need food to live, but we largely live off of the spiritual energy we receive from the other world. That is why you cannot go on without recharging this energy. Therefore, I recommend that those who are spiritually sensitive sleep early and get enough rest.

Also, try to take it easy on the weekend and rest your body. Set aside at least one day of the week for the Sabbath— in other words, a time of rest. During that day, stay home, read books, or listen to music instead of going out. Try to have a quiet day once a week, and you can be active for the rest of the week.

If you think you are one of those people who get tired easily, you should set aside a day to recharge yourself and avoid interacting with others. You can work hard the other six days. Then, rest for a day again. Try to control your lifestyle by setting this cycle. This is important. Being tired easily will always be part of your life, so accept it and take control of it.

Dealing with stress that comes from interpersonal relations

To add one more thing, I understand it will be tough if your coworker or someone you meet often has negative vibrations. It must be very difficult to sit side-by-side at work every day with someone who is possessed by as many as five evil spirits. The person being possessed must be having a hard time, but you will be too. If you are in that situation, please pray to your guardian spirit and ask for a more suitable environment. Please pray for a suitable environment with no harm done to anyone. If you do, you will soon be given a different setting, or the person you are having trouble with will go somewhere else. Sometimes, you need to offer this kind of prayer.

Perhaps you have a so-called friend who is quite audacious and will intrude into your personal space with no concern for your feelings. He or she will keep crossing the line if you stay quiet. Some people in this world are quite egoistic in this way.

To deal with these people, you must keep your distance from them, and when they cross your boundaries, sometimes you must take a strict attitude and shut them out. When they overstep your boundaries or invade too much of your privacy, you must confront them and tell them that you don't want them to meddle with certain things or you don't intend to get too close to them. It is important that you make yourself clear at least once. Then, when they get close to crossing the line again, they will realize it and take a step back because they don't want to be confronted again.

Interestingly, these audacious people care about others' opinions more than you'd think. So once they know your boundaries, they will remember them and keep their distance from you. If you are struggling with their bold behavior, take a strict attitude and tell them how you feel. You do not actually have to be angry or hate them; just tell yourself that you are acting. Play the role of a stern and strict person, and they will know that you have a tough side and back down.

Therefore, spiritual beings are not the only concern. People's will and people's thoughts also come into play. No one wants to be disliked by others. Whether you are a good or bad person, you do not want others to dislike you. That, in a way, helps the world work smoothly. So sometimes it is important to show your feelings.

You shouldn't let others do more evil due to your ignorance. For this reason, you should observe people and keep a good distance when interacting with them.

Women need to rest in advance, whereas men need to be told to rest

Other than what I mentioned above, you must get enough rest. In particular, women should rest before they get tired instead of after, as they generally have less stamina than men. When you feel you are starting to lose energy, rest. It is like a preventive measure.

For example, if you think you might argue with your husband on a particular night, take a nap during the day. Take a nap and recharge your energy if you think you will be "hit by a storm" on that night. If you have enough energy, you will be able to endure the storm without easily losing your temper, but if you are tired, you will become emotional, and things can get out of hand. Thus, women need rest to prevent or prepare for what's to come. If you feel you are getting tired, please rest.

On the other hand, men tend to only rest after they have overexerted themselves. They go too far and only rest just before they collapse. So if you are a married woman, please tell your husband to rest and relax earlier than that.

People, especially men, find it hard to know when to rest. They hesitate to say they need time off because they are afraid of being seen as incompetent. That is why it helps when someone else tells them to rest. Caring words by the wife reassure the husband; that is what men are waiting for. Therefore, the wife should tell her husband to rest.

Please refer to what I have mentioned today.

CHAPTER FOUR

Spread the Truth
and Save the People

1

Guiding People Who Have Negative Vibrations

Q1

I often had difficulties dealing with people who had negative vibrations, so after much consideration, I decided to join Happy Science. I want to build a stronger self to repel evil spirits and negative vibrations of people, but I also want to be kind enough to help and guide them. In order to become a person of this caliber, what points should I keep in mind as I practice my daily disciplines, such as self-reflection and meditation?

The Second Special Seminar of 1990,
"A Lecture on the Methods of Meditation—Meditation of the Great Ocean,"
held on July 22, 1990, at Takatsuki City Hall in Osaka, Japan

---

Three sources of energy

OK, that is quite a difficult problem. In fact, what you are trying to do is an eternal challenge. Our lecturers are also facing this exact problem. The level of this problem may vary, but there is no end to its difficulty. I am facing the same problem, too.

Undoubtedly, it requires enormous energy to guide people and change their bad vibrations into good ones. If people with weak energy attempt to do this, they will suffer serious repercussions. So we must increase our energy first.

The three energy sources of humans are physical stamina, intellectual power, and willpower. These are the three elements of our energy. In terms of physical stamina, it varies from person to person. But you can also improve it through training. This is one source.

Efforts you need to make to be able to give "prescriptions" quickly

Another source is intellectual power. If you have high intellectual power, it means you can quickly reach a conclusion on how to solve other people's problems. You can get to the crucial point of the problem someone is facing, so you do not have to fall into any unnecessary argument with the person. You can quickly give "prescriptions" for their problem. As your intellectual power increases, you will be able to promptly tell which prescription will yield which result. You can reach a conclusion in a short time.

The same applies to surgeons. Good surgeons will quickly determine the affected area and operate on it. But what if a surgeon operated on you many times without being able to identify where exactly you are affected? That would be unbearable.

Surgery succeeds because the doctor can accurately identify and operate on the lesion. Precision in surgery shows how good of a doctor you are. Trial and error does not work in surgery. Surgeons who make these kinds of mistakes should preferably resign.

The same applies when solving people's problems. People with high intellectual power can point out the very cause of the problems others are facing in their life. Simply put, just by pointing out the cause, people can change, and you do not have to exert all your energy.

There are several reasons why people seem bad or emit evil vibrations. You must determine which reason is the core problem. Once you identify what it is, you only need to tackle that. There is no need to change those people entirely. If you focus on and think about how to change the part that is causing them to have negative vibrations, you will find the most efficient method for them to overcome their problem. You do not have to struggle so much to help people if you can do this efficiently and effortlessly.

To gain such abilities, you need intellectual power. To improve your intellectual power, you must, of course, study the books of Truth, but you must also be cultured in terms of general knowledge. You must have expert knowledge in your field of work, too. People generally tend to accept what experts tell them but get annoyed if they are preached by those who don't have much skills. That is why you also need intellectual power.

How to train your willpower

There is also willpower, which you can strengthen through training. To train your willpower, you must put yourself in a situation where you are required to work beyond your abilities. Your willpower will grow by actively taking on jobs or positions beyond your current abilities.

Today, I am standing here on the stage and speaking to you all for two hours, which is quite easy for me to do. On the other hand, if I pointed to someone in the audience and asked him or her to come onto the stage to give a speech, I think they would panic; just thinking about it might make them nervous and sweaty.

However, once they actually come up here, they might surprisingly be able to do it. Usually, people make a big fuss about taking on a challenge before trying, but they will never strengthen their willpower if they back away from it.

I'm sure some of you will be asked to take on roles as you partake in Happy Science activities. You might be asked to be a team leader, to be a district leader, or to take part in an activity. Some may think that declining the offer because they feel they aren't capable enough makes them humble and respectable. But when such an offer comes, please be courageous and accept it, even if you think you can't do it. You might be surprised that you can actually do it. In this way, you should continue to take on challenges by accepting new offers. This will strengthen your willpower.

Therefore, to improve your willpower, you should actively accept challenges that you think are beyond your current abilities. Train yourself to say "yes" instead of saying "no." Rather than declining the offer, say, "Let me try" or "I will think about it." Always try to face the challenge with a positive attitude, and soon, you will be able to work with full willpower.

Please make a conscious effort to polish your physical stamina, intellectual power, and willpower every day. By training and polishing them little by little, eventually, the total amount of your energy increases, which will give you much power to guide various types of people.

There is no other way to do this but to train yourself every day. This is true for everyone, including myself. Let's all do our best.

2

Conveying the Truth to People Who Believe in a Misguided Religion

---

Q2

You have taught us various ways to convey the Truth to people who believe in a misguided religion. One of the ways is to hand them a book of Truth. But what if the person you want to convey the Truth to lives far away and you rarely have the chance to meet them in person? What can I do to help them realize they believe in a misguided religion?

The Seventh Thursday Seminar, "What Is Spiritual Channeling?" held on November 24, 1988, at Happy Science Training Hall in Nishi-Ogikubo, Tokyo, Japan

---

The simple way to convey the Truth to someone who lives far away

I believe there are different ways to convey the Truth depending on the situation. If the person you want to convey the Truth to lives far away, the simplest way is to wait for the right opportunity. Sometimes, all you can do is wait for the right moment. Some people are just not interested in learning the Truth yet. Even if you give them one of our books, they will either throw it away or laugh at it, so it's no good. They will just make fun of you.

But even for those people, life is not always smooth; things do not always work out. They will go through ups and downs, and indeed, there will be turning points in their lives. Things won't always turn out well; people will also experience hardships. For example, you may go through financial distress, become ill, or experience misfortunes in the family such as the loss of your child or spouse. All kinds of things happen in life.

Humans are meant to experience adversities at some point in their life. There is no doubt. So wait for the right time. If you think that now is the time, you should talk to them about the Truth. If not, you can watch over them quietly and hope they will eventually turn out for the better. This is also an act of love.

Timing is important because people cannot accept the teachings unless the time is right. I myself feel that I might have laughed at my books if it wasn't for the right timing. I have turned to religion and spirituality because I met them at the right time. Otherwise, I wouldn't have been interested in religion. I believe so.

Everyone has their own timing to awaken to the Truth. If you think their time is close, you should tell them the

Truth. If you think their time is much later, you should wait for the right time. You can focus on someone else who needs the teachings now instead. You should tell the Truth to those who are more in need.

The reason we fill bookstores with the books of Truth

You will also find many atheists and materialists among the general public. I believe it is Happy Science's great mission to spread the Truth and enlighten them all.

Many people in society do not believe in the existence of the Spirit World, so I am trying to show them proof. Two or three of my books are published every month, and about 29 books will be published this year (at the time of this lecture), but you will know that this is impossible to do if you consider how long it usually takes to write and publish books. This is one way to prove the existence of the Spirit World. Intellectual people understand how impossible it is to write and publish books at this pace.

What makes it possible? They are none other than revelations from the heavenly world. There is no way I can write this many books without receiving revelations from heaven. I am deliberately filling bookstores with the books of Truth as proof.

I also have other strategies in mind. IRH Press, which is Happy Science's publishing company, will officially be in full swing next year. We were still working on establishing the organizational structure of Happy Science, namely the secretariat division, so our publishing company was still on hold (at the time of the lecture). It will move into full gear starting next year (Note). IRH Press is now set up; we opened its bank account and prepared other things, so we are ready to go. Although it is up to each individual to realize the Truth, we will run publicity campaigns to provide opportunities for them to do so. It is our job to give many people the chance to encounter the Truth.

Happy Science as an organization will aim to convey the Truth to a large number of people, so you can be part of our movement. At an individual level, please look out for the right time for each person, as I mentioned above. Wait until the right time, and prioritize those who are in need now. For those who are not quite ready, please wait for the right time to come.

(Note) Since 1991, IRH Press, Co. has published a series of books by Ryuho Okawa and has consecutively produced bestsellers for over 30 years (research done by two major publication distributors in Japan: Tohan and Nippan). In 2011, Okawa set a new world record for the number of books published in bookstores by a single author in one year—52 books. The record was certified by Guinness World Records. In 2014, Okawa published 161 books in a single year. As of July 2023, the total number of books published has surpassed 3,100.

3

Faith of Newly Converted Happy Science Members

Q3

My question is about faith. For someone who used to be an avid believer of another new religion but realized its teachings were false and converted to Happy Science, it is truly difficult to have 100 percent faith in Happy Science's teachings. Can you please give them advice from both personal and general perspectives?

The First Public Lecture of 1990, "Faith and Love,"
held on March 11, 1990, at Makuhari Messe in Chiba, Japan

Reflect on why you believed in false teachings

First, I will answer in terms of the personal aspect. Such kinds of people have a hard time believing Happy Science's teachings because they have a strong sense of betrayal. You know what it's like to be betrayed. What they had believed to be 100 percent true turned out to be zero percent true. In a way, it is natural for humans to develop a strong sense of betrayal after experiencing something like that.

However, before they feel betrayed, they should think about why they fell for those false teachings in the first place. What was it that drew them to such teachings? There was something within them that attracted them to those teachings. They must find out what it is. They shouldn't just blame the false teachings. Instead, they should take this experience as a chance to reflect on themselves and learn something from it. If they can manage to do that, they will, in turn, be able to tell what are real teachings.

After all, people like them tend to have a sense of guilt, but because they cannot be honest and admit what they have done, they seek redemption by joining a new religion. This is the most common mistake they make. Quite a few people who join a misguided religion are like that. They are drawn to that religion to seek forgiveness for their sins. Therefore, I must say that such people have a mistaken way of thinking.

From the standpoint of Happy Science, they, themselves, are the only ones who can correct their wrong thoughts or actions. If they don't do it themselves, no one else will. Needless to say, they cannot be forgiven just by carrying a cross, writing their name as part of a ritual, or praying.

So these people should examine themselves thoroughly to see if they joined a misguided religion to seek forgiveness at their own convenience.

How to determine if a religion is right or wrong

To distinguish whether a religion is right or wrong from a general perspective, let me refer to the parable of Jesus, "A tree is known by its fruit," which is related to what I mentioned above. Looking at the past 2,000 years of history, this seems to be the best way to determine whether something is good or bad.

You will know what kind of "tree" a religion is by checking the "fruit" it bears, meaning that you can determine whether a religion is good or bad by looking at how its believers turn out to be. If many of them become respectable and great after learning its teachings, then it is a good religion. On the other hand, if they become more and more odd, then you should think that the "tree" itself is rotten.

Now, the question is, how can you determine for yourself whether your judgment of whether a religion is right or misguided is credible? To do this, you must become honest with yourself and ask your own heart.

We all have a subconscious layer in our minds that is connected to our guardian spirits. By removing all your vanity and personal interests, you can quietly converse with your mind. Reflect on yourself before making judgments. Decide whether those people seem wonderful or not in your eyes.

If they are in fact odd but seem wonderful in your eyes, then you will end up in the same world as them after you die, regardless of whether you join their religion. You will have to take responsibility for your judgments. You will have to take the risk yourself in the end. That is why it's important that you seriously ask yourself and determine if the religion is right or not. Needless to say, a religious group should have many cheerful and happy members. This is an important point.

Another checkpoint is to see whether the religious group is reasonably tolerant and allows its members to think sensibly to a certain level. Beware of religious groups that demand their followers to uphold a unified ideology and prohibit anything else. Such an idea can be right at times, but if taken in the wrong way, it can become a dangerous ideology. A religious group should have reasonable codes, meaning it should be tolerant to some extent. You should also check whether the followers are allowed to think sensibly to a certain degree.

4

Guiding Someone Who Seeks
the Meaning of Life

Q4

I only recently became a Happy Science member and have just begun to study the Truth. The other day, I tried to convey the Truth to one of my coworkers. He asked me, "Why should we refine our souls?" So I told him, "Because it will make us happy." He understood what I said. He then asked me another question: "Then, what is my raison d'être in this world?" I wasn't prepared for this question and couldn't answer him very well. How can I answer him better?

The Ninth Public Lecture of 1990, "The Enlightenment of the Great Universe," held on August 26, 1990, at Makuhari Messe in Chiba, Japan

Some people need
a concrete explanation of the teachings

So far, we have published nearly 100 books (at the time of this lecture; as of July 2023, over 3,100 books have been published), and in fact, they are all filled with answers; all of my books contain answers. So I suggest you bring your coworker to one of the seminars conducted by our lecturers in the local branches and have the lecturer talk to him one on one. It seems that your coworker is the type of person who needs a concrete explanation, not abstract ideas.

You have to guide him through the teachings. For example, you can explain it to him in this way: "You are this type of person, and you are suffering from this particular issue. You would be happy if it turned out like this, right? Now, what I'm saying is written here in this book. I think you would be happier if you could accept this way of thinking." Then, he will understand.

Some people will never understand the Truth unless you point it out to them clearly. They won't understand a thing even if you begin by explaining to them the origin of the universe. These people need to be told clearly.

If you want to tell your coworker the meaning of living a happy life, you need to stop thinking in an abstract manner. Instead, you should pay close attention to him and learn what he is struggling with, so you can tell him what he needs to do to change himself. Everyone has something they are struggling with. We all carry at least a problem or two. So what you can do is find the "pin" stuck in them that is causing their problem. As soon as this pin is removed, they will change, so you must find it. The process of finding the pin and removing it is taught in our teachings in various ways, so you should help your coworker find his pin.

Most people do not realize that they have a pin stuck in them. They do not know much about themselves. They think their way of thinking is only natural, but so many people in this world think differently. When your thinking changes, the world you see changes significantly.

I gave a lecture in May this year (1990) in Hiroshima titled "Rebuilding Your Life" (to be included in *Best Selection of Ryuho Okawa's Early Lectures Vol. 4*). I discussed many general topics that people can relate to. The tape of this lecture will be coming out soon, so please have your friend listen to it (now available as a DVD video). That is one thing you can do for him.

I also held a lecture titled "Living in Eternity Now" (to be included in *Best Selection of Ryuho Okawa's Early Lectures Vol. 5*) in Nagoya in July. This was mainly about the theory of time, but I also discussed how much merit there is in living while knowing the purpose and mission of your life. Even people in the business world should be able to understand this lecture, so please share it with him as well.

There are many people like him. I have been giving all kinds of teachings, little by little, so that people can find the teaching that best applies to them. Please refer to those teachings.

5

Guiding People
Who Are New to the Truth

Q5

My question is about how to guide people who are new to the Truth. I know someone who is a member of Happy Science who says learning the Truth is wonderful and wishes to become a bodhisattva. He understands that he cannot become a bodhisattva without putting what he learns into practice. He is passionate about the movement for salvation and is willing to put his life on the line. However, his enthusiasm is not accompanied by his actions. I would like to ask for your advice as I truly wish to guide him. What kind of mindset should I have when I talk to him? Is there an effective or decisive move I should keep in mind?

The May Seminar of 1992, "The Mission of Angels,"
held on April 22, 1992, at Happy Science Headquarters, Kioicho Office,
in Tokyo, Japan

The daily discipline you must do
if you aspire to guide others

The answer is simple. It all comes down to whether you truly understand the other person. People often become too enthusiastic and assertive before they fully understand a person. When you think you are working hard and passionately, you are usually being forceful. Therefore, you should check whether you are being a high-pressure seller.

People have different starting points. Some are behind, and some are ahead. So you must be able to understand their current state of mind, where they are in their spiritual development, the amount of learning they have done, and so forth. In particular, those who are young and passionately want to spread the Truth tend to suffer in this regard. After all, it is not other people's fault for not understanding what these young people are trying to convey but instead their own fault for not being able to see the other person's state of mind.

On the other hand, older people have an overwhelming advantage in this area. They are, in a way, experts in understanding others. They can tell what kind of person someone is overall. It is like being able to tell the nature of a tree: whether the branch is crooked, the trunk is crooked, or the leaves have often been diseased. Older people can instantly recognize such things, but younger people cannot, which is why they struggle.

However, this is also an opportunity given to you to take on life's challenges through missionary work. You are not enlightened enough to save others entirely, but you are also being saved at the same time. You are given an opportunity to learn as you convey the Truth to others. This is where you stand.

As I said, being able to understand others is all that matters. For instance, you cannot communicate with someone with little or limited vocabulary, even if you try. Even for me, there was a time when a weekly magazine interviewed me but I couldn't talk about the Truth at all. When I used my spiritual sight, I saw that the interviewer's head was completely empty; he had nothing in his head. There was a hollow cylinder in his head, an open space. If this space reached all the way up to heaven, then that would have been quite impressive; but that was not the case. So I had no choice but to speak about worldly matters, as I could see and understand he had nothing in his head. Still, I thought it was better than not doing the interview. It is a part of my job to leave some kind of an impression on others, even if it is in the slightest.

There is no point in rushing, as there are various kinds of people. For example, I mentioned the Buddhist concept of the "Ten Worlds" in today's lecture ("The Mission of Angels"). People with no spiritual knowledge won't be able to understand a thing about this concept. It's a matter of course that they will just end up becoming lost.

On top of that, even after you begin studying the Truth, it usually takes about three years to get a good understanding of it. You may think you understand it or even score 100 or 99 percent on the Truth Exam, sometimes by cramming for two or three months. But this does not prove that you understand the Truth fully. It takes at least three years of studying the Truth to grasp the true meaning of it. Even then, you still have a long, long way to go to understand the Truth.

Are you able to tell what kind of person someone is? How much you can see other people's character, state of mind, personal history, experience, and personality depends on your daily discipline. This applies to everything.

Take kendo, for example. When you stand in a *dojo* with a *shinai* (bamboo sword), you check the swordsmanship of your opponent by observing their moves, such as how they tap and swing the shinai. When you become more advanced, you can tell what the opponent's ability is like just by tapping the end of each other's shinai once or twice. You don't need to see the opponent's swing. You will be struck by them if you can only tell this after they make a move.

If your opponent is not at the same level as you, you can often tell whether you will win or lose by tapping the tip of each other's shinai and observing their fighting spirit, their gaze, and how they keep their distance. If they are at the same level as yours, you cannot, but if there is a gap in skill, usually the outcome is obvious the moment you become poised.

Even in sports, skill levels vary from player to player, so you can imagine the many stages of mental discipline, such as black belt and white belt. Therefore, you have no choice but to keep polishing your skills. To do so, you will need to interact with various types of people and learn the different patterns. Also, you should interact and have a good relationship with older people. Then, they will share their wisdom on how to see and think about things and how to perceive others.

On the other hand, older people should interact with those about 30 years younger, as younger people can stimulate their intellect. It would be good for them to hold study sessions with people 30 years younger on a regular basis. By interacting with the young ones, older people can stimulate their intellect and get a sense of the new age. Those who are younger should study with older people to learn how to perceive people and society. In this way, please learn from the study sessions held at Happy Science.

So you need to accept this fact: it is about being able to tell how skilled your "opponent" is, like the kendo example I mentioned above. At times, you could be the one to be struck.

I will leave it at that.

6

How to Live Beautifully in an Age Overflowing with Malicious Information

Q6

You taught us that the age of Hermes in ancient Greece was a time when men and women lived most beautifully. I'm sure the situation now is different from back then, with satanic information overflowing in our society. Still, I would like to live beautifully in the current age. What ideal should we pursue, and how should we live our lives? Please teach us.

The End-of-Year Special Seminar, "Lecture on *The Eternal Buddha*," held on December 8, 1991, at Nakano Fujimicho Olympic Building in Tokyo, Japan

Looking at modern society from a spiritual eye

The current generation perceives today's society as extremely advanced and developed, but that is the world seen through a physical eye. Seen through a spiritual eye, this world is like a house with pillars that are being swarmed by termites and are about to collapse. That is how this world appears to me, but it seems that people are calling this "progress."

An age when termites infest pillars is not a beautiful age. I imagine a beautiful age to be something like animals hopping around joyfully in a prairie. I feel that the age of Hermes in ancient Greece resembled that. On the contrary, modern society looks more like termites moving frantically with no individuality.

Purifying people's minds in modern society

There are two ways to purify modern society. One is to reduce the population by natural disasters. The other is for people to learn the Right Teaching. Even if people live together in a tight space, we can live beautifully without intruding on each other by learning the Right Teaching.

If we are struck with full-scale natural disasters, where land sinks here and there and many people die, there is a high chance that the world will return to an agricultural society. But I'm not entirely against it because it will be a new starting point, in a sense. On the other hand, if we wish to improve modern society while keeping it alive, we must change the world, starting with education. We must also eliminate a significant amount of the hellish influences rampant on earth, including people's basic lifestyles.

The mass media plays a large role in spreading poison in modern society, and they are supported by a large number of "termite-like" people. Both factors influence society in a negative way. There is a jumble of not-so-good information in this world that enters us through our eyes and ears, and it is eating away at our minds in a substantial way.

Making this world wonderful

The world will become a wonderful place if it is filled with people who accept God's teachings smoothly and properly, with a pure heart. To create such a world, religion must spread as a fundamental part of society.

In that respect, Buddha's Truth that Happy Science teaches must stand above the national law. Buddha's Truth is more precious than the national law, the constitution, laws created by a king, or the rules of society. It stands above these things. It transcends age and country. The world will not become better unless countries and societies are built upon the Eternal Truth.

The laws in this world are created by sixth-dimensional-level experts in law at best, who rack their brains to create them. They cannot understand anything beyond their level. They are clueless about the World of Love and the World of Mercy. Unless people understand that there are nobler, eternal teachings, they cannot build a society of this quality.

People now cannot even tell accurately or clearly what is good and what is evil, or what is heavenly and what is hellish. So I believe it all depends on how quickly and deeply we can reach into people's hearts with our activities. If we do not succeed, humanity might face many dire consequences. That's how it will be.

There is no other way than to have people understand the Truth. We need to make studying the Truth common sense. We need to create a world where everyone studies the Truth at home, at school, and even after becoming adults. The Truth should make its way into people's hearts directly. Everyone should know that Buddha's Truth is far more holy than any of the laws of this world. To make a better world is to build a world based on Buddha's Truth. There is no other way.

If a religious group or its leader who teaches Buddha's Truth is criticized by magazines that print nude photos, and if people support those magazines, the entire world will end. Their country will have to disappear into the sea; that will be its destiny. An incident like that must be prevented. That is why there is a big battle of values going on.

It is about time people know which side is closer to God and which side is closer to Satan. The time is coming when we will establish order. If we cannot accomplish this mission while we are still alive, a long battle will follow. My disciples will be born and persecuted again and again over many lives, for hundreds or thousands of years. Perhaps that might be "exciting" for some people, so I won't protest against it. Anyhow, all we can do is do our best.

Afterword

Some of you may have been spiritually sensitive since birth or may have become spiritually sensitive after encountering Buddha's Truth.

It has been about 30 years since the Q&A sessions compiled in this volume took place. Over those years, we have seen many incidents occur one after another—various illnesses have been cured, and our ritual prayers and other prayers have worked miracles.

In a way, my spiritual abilities have significantly grown, and Happy Science has grown bigger and stronger as an organization.

If you are suffering from spiritual disturbances right now, first, you should check whether you are an egoist or not. Egoistic people can lead a peaceful life if their work and their capability are well-balanced or if they are blessed with a caring coworker. However, at some point, you will face obstacles or encounter hardships because you lack knowledge and experience, and you will most likely fall into panic. That is when you will unexpectedly suffer from spiritual phenomena or disturbances.

First, observe your mind as if looking at a mirror, and live an orderly life. Remind yourself every morning, "Today, I will sow at least one seed of happiness."

Sometimes, thinking about a life of desiring little and knowing contentment is important.

If you only seek worldly success, your life can be full of suffering. But if you see life as an opportunity to gain precious spiritual experience, your world is filled with light.

Ryuho Okawa
Master & CEO of Happy Science Group
September 28, 2021

For a deeper understanding of
The Truth about Spiritual Phenomena: Life's Q&A with El Cantare
see other books below by Ryuho Okawa:

The Laws of Success [New York: IRH Press, 2017]
Invincible Thinking [New York: IRH Press, 2017]

ABOUT THE AUTHOR

Founder and CEO of Happy Science Group.

Ryuho Okawa was born on July 7th 1956, in Tokushima, Japan. After graduating from the University of Tokyo with a law degree, he joined a Tokyo-based trading house. While working at its New York headquarters, he studied international finance at the Graduate Center of the City University of New York. In 1981, he attained Great Enlightenment and became aware that he is El Cantare with a mission to bring salvation to all humankind.

In 1986, he established Happy Science. It now has members in 169 countries across the world, with more than 700 branches and temples as well as 10,000 missionary houses around the world.

He has given over 3,500 lectures (of which more than 150 are in English) and published over 3,100 books (of which more than 600 are Spiritual Interview Series), and many of them are translated into 41 languages. Along with *The Laws of the Sun* and *The Laws of Hell*, many of the books have become best sellers or million sellers. To date, Happy Science has produced 27 movies under the supervision of Okawa. He has given the original story and concept and is also the Executive Producer. He has also composed music and written lyrics of over 450 pieces.

Moreover, he is the Founder of Happy Science University and Happy Science Academy (Junior and Senior High School), Founder and President of the Happiness Realization Party, Founder and Honorary Headmaster of Happy Science Institute of Government and Management, Founder of IRH Press Co., Ltd., and the Chairperson of NEW STAR PRODUCTION Co., Ltd. and ARI Production Co., Ltd.

BOOKS BY RYUHO OKAWA

The Power of Salvation to Resolve Spiritual Disturbances:
Happy Science Books and Music

Ryuho Okawa has disclosed the existence of invisible beings such as the spirits of ancestors, stray spirits, and evil spirits that causes various spiritual disturbances. To help people resolve such disturbances, he continues to publish various kinds of books. He also writes and composes music that contains the power of Buddha's Truth, which has worked many miracles: the COVID-positive patients testing negative, sleep paralysis being resolved, deafness with an unknown cause being cured, etc.

The Spiritual Truth About Curses and Spells

How to Get Out of an Unhappy Life

Paperback • 140 pages • $14.95
ISBN: 979-8-88737-062-0 (Sep. 28, 2022)

Curses may be the reason for your unhappiness. Curses are nothing special but something that occurs in daily life; this is the Spiritual Truth. Our feelings of jealousy and anger can be transmitted as thoughts of curses and cause harm to others, or they can be repelled back and bring misfortune to the person who gave the curse. This is a unique book like no other; it tells you the method to protect yourself from such curses and stop the cursing that brings unhappiness to yourself and others.

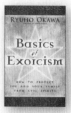

Basics of Exorcism

How to Protect You and Your Family
from Evil Spirits

Paperback • 130 pages • $14.95
ISBN: 979-8887370408 (Aug. 12, 2022)

No matter how much time progresses, demons are real. Spiritual screen against curses – the truth of exorcism as told by the author who possesses the six great supernatural powers – The essence of exorcism as a result of more than 5,000 rounds of exorcist experience!

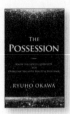

The Possession
Know the Ghost Condition and Overcome Negative Spiritual Influence
Paperback • 114 pages • $14.95
ISBN: 979-8887370033 (Jun. 11, 2022)

Possession is neither an exceptional occurrence nor unscientific superstition; it's a phenomenon, based on spiritual principles, that is still quite common in the modern society. Through this book, you can find the way to change your own mind and free yourself from possession, and the way to exorcise devils by relying on the power of angels and God.

The Real Exorcist
Attain Wisdom to Conquer Evil
Paperback • 208 pages • $16.95
ISBN:978-1-942125-67-9 (Jun. 15, 2020)

This is a profound spiritual text backed by the author's nearly 40 years of real-life experience with spiritual phenomena. In it, Okawa teaches how we may discern and overcome our negative tendencies, by acquiring the right knowledge, mindset and lifestyle.

Healing Power
The True Mechanism of Mind and Illness
Paperback • 190 pages • $14.95
ISBN: 979-8-88737-048-4 (Aug. 26, 2022)

This book describes the relationship between the mind and illness, and provides you with hints to restore your mental and physical health. By reading this book, you can find tips on how to heal your body from illnesses such as cancer, heart disease, allergy, skin disease, dementia, psychiatric disorder, and atopy. You will gain the miraculous power of healing.

CD

—— The Thunder ——
a composition for repelling the Coronavirus

We have been granted this music from our Lord. It will repel away the novel Coronavirus originated in China. Experience this magnificent powerful music.

Search on YouTube

the thunder composition for a short ad!

El Cantare Trilogy

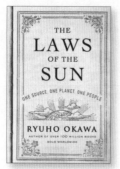

The Laws of the Sun

One Source, One Planet, One People

Paperback • 288 pages • $15.95
ISBN: 978-1-942125-43-3 (Oct. 25, 2018)

Imagine if you could ask God why he created this world and what spiritual laws he used to shape us—and everything around us. Ryuho Okawa outlines these laws of the universe and provides a road map for living one's life with greater purpose and meaning. This powerful book shows the way to realize true happiness—a happiness that continues from this world through the other.

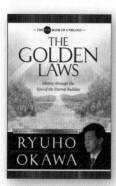

The Golden Laws

History through the Eyes of the Eternal Buddha

E-book • 204 pages • $13.99
ISBN: 978-1-941779-82-8 (Sep. 24, 2015)

Throughout history, Great Guiding Spirits of Light have been present on Earth in both the East and the West at crucial points in human history to further our spiritual development. *The Golden Laws* reveals how Divine Plan has been unfolding on Earth, and outlines 5,000 years of the secret history of humankind.

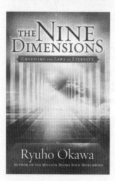

The Nine Dimensions

Unveiling the Laws of Eternity

Paperback • 168 pages • $15.95
ISBN: 978-0-982698-56-3 (Feb. 16, 2012)

This book is a window into the mind of our loving God. When the religions and cultures of the world discover the truth of their common spiritual origin, they will be inspired to accept their differences, come together under faith in God, and build an era of harmony and peaceful progress on Earth.

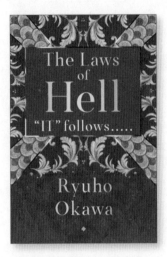

The Laws of Hell

"IT" follows.....

Paperback • 264 pages • $17.95
ISBN: 978-1-958655-04-7 (May 1, 2023)

Whether you believe it or not, the Spirit World and hell do exist. Currently, the Earth's population has exceeded 8 billion, and unfortunately, 1 in 2 people are falling to hell.

This book is a must-read at a time like this since more and more people are unknowingly heading to hell; the truth is, new areas of hell are being created, such as 'internet hell' and 'hell on earth.' Also, due to the widespread materialism, there is a sharp rise in the earthbound spirits wandering around Earth because they have no clue about the Spirit World.

To stop hell from spreading and to save the souls of all human beings, the Spiritual Master, Ryuho Okawa has compiled vital teachings in this book. This publication marks his 3,100th book and is the one and only comprehensive Truth about the modern hell.

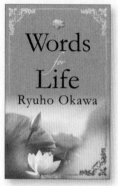

Words for Life

Paperback • 136 pages • $15.95
ISBN: 979-8-88727-089-7 (Mar. 16, 2023)

Ryuho Okawa has written over 3,100 books on various topics. To help readers find the teachings that are beneficial for them out of the extensive teachings, the author has written 100 phrases and put them together in this book. Inside you will find words of wisdom that will help you improve your mindset and lead you to live a meaningful and happy life.

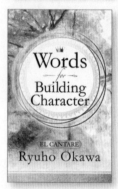

Words for Building Character

Paperback • 140 pages • $15.95
ISBN: 979-8-88737-091-0 (Jun. 21, 2023)

As you read this book, you will discover the wisdom to build a noble character through various life experiences. When your life comes to an end, what you can bring with you to the other world is, in Buddhism terms, enlightenment, and in other words, it is the character that you build in this lifetime. If you can read, relish, and truly understand the meaning of these religious phrases, you will be able to attain happiness that transcends this world and the next.

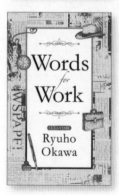

Words for Work

Paperback • 140 pages • $15.95
ISBN: 979-8-88737-090-3 (Jul. 20, 2023)

Through his personal experiences at work and receiving inspiration from God and the angels in the heavenly world, Okawa has created these phrases regarding philosophies and practical wisdom about work. Have this book on your desk and it will be of great use to you throughout your career. Every day you can contemplate and gain tips on how to better your work as well as deepen your insight into company management.

Healing Books

Words to Read in Times of Illness

Paperback • 136 pages • $17.95
ISBN: 978-1-958655-07-8 (Sep. 15, 2023)

Ryuho Okawa's 100 Healing Messages of Light with the spiritual truths to comfort the souls of those going through any illness. Okawa indicates that when we are ill, it is an ideal time for us to recall and contemplate recent and past events, as well as our relationship with people around us. It is a chance for us to take inventory of our emotions and thoughts buried during our busy everyday life.

Healing from Within

Life-Changing Keys to Calm, Spiritual, and Healthy Living

Paperback • 208 pages • $15.95
ISBN:978-1-942125-18-1 (Jun. 30, 2017)

None of us wants to become sick, but why is it that we can't avoid illness in life? Is there a meaning behind illness? In this book, Ryuho Okawa reveals the true causes and remedies for various illnesses that modern medicine doesn't know how to heal. Building a happier and healthier life starts with believing in the power of our mind and understanding the relationship between mind and body.

Worry-Free Living

Let Go of Stress and
Live in Peace and Happiness

Hardcover • 192 pages • $16.95
ISBN: 978-1-942125-51-8 (May 15, 2019)

The wisdom Ryuho Okawa shares in this book about facing problems in human relationships, financial hardships, and other life's stresses will help you change how you look at and approach life's worries and problems for the better. Let this book be your guide to finding precious meaning in all your life's problems, gaining inner growth and practicing inner happiness and spiritual growth.

New Books

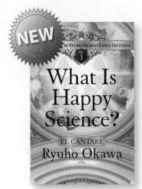

What Is Happy Science?

Best Selection of Ryuho Okawa's Early Lectures (Volume 1)

Paperback • 256 pages • $17.95
ISBN: 978-1-942125-99-0 (Jul. 1, 2023)

The Best Selection series is a collection of Ryuho Okawa's passionate lectures during the ages of 32 to 33 that reveal the mission and goal of Happy Science. This book contains the eternal Truth, including the meaning of life, the secret of the mind, the true meaning of love, the mystery of the universe, and how to end hatred and world conflicts.

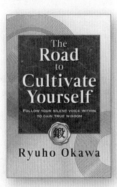

The Road to Cultivate Yourself

Follow Your Silent Voice Within to Gain True Wisdom

Paperback • 256 pages • $17.95
ISBN: 978-1-958655-05-4 (Jun. 22, 2023)

What is the ideal way of living when chaos and destruction are accelerated?

This book offers unchanging Truth in the ever-changing world, such as the secrets to become more aware about the spiritual self and how to increase intellectual productivity amidst the rapid changes of the modern age. It is packed with Ryuho Okawa's crystallized wisdom of life.

The Challenge of Enlightenment

Now, Here, the New Dharma Wheel Turns

Paperback • 380 pages • $17.95
ISBN: 978-1-942125-92-1 (Dec. 20, 2022)

Buddha's teachings, a reflection of his eternal wisdom, are like a bamboo pole used to change the course of your boat in the rapid stream of the great river called life. By reading this book, your mind becomes clearer, learns to savor inner peace, and it will empower you to make profound life improvements.

Bestselling Buddhist Titles

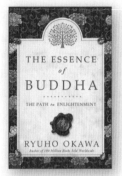

The Essence of Buddha

The Path to Enlightenment

Paperback • 208 pages • $14.95
ISBN: 978-1-942125-06-8 (Oct. 1, 2016)

The essence of Shakyamuni Buddha's original teachings of the mind are explained in simple language: how to attain inner happiness, the wisdom to conquer ego, and the path to enlightenment for people in the contemporary era. It is a way of life that anyone can practice to achieve lifelong self-growth.

The Challenge of the Mind

An Essential Guide to Buddha's Teachings: Zen, Karma and Enlightenment

Paperback • 208 pages • $16.95
ISBN: 978-1-942125-45-7 (Nov. 15, 2018)

In this book, Ryuho Okawa explains essential Buddhist tenets and how to put them into practice. Enlightenment is not just an abstract idea but one that everyone can experience to some extent. Okawa offers a solid basis of reason and intellectual understanding to Buddhist concepts.

The True Eightfold Path

Guideposts for Self-Innovation

Paperback • 256 pages • $16.95
ISBN: 978-1-942125-80-8 (Mar. 30, 2021)

This book explains how we can apply the Eightfold Path, one of the main pillars of Shakyamuni Buddha's teachings, as everyday guideposts in the modern-age to achieve self-innovation to live better and make positive changes in these uncertain times.

WHO IS EL CANTARE?

El Cantare means "the Light of the Earth." He is the Supreme God of the Earth who has been guiding humankind since the beginning of Genesis, and He is the Creator of the universe. He is whom Jesus called Father and Muhammad called Allah, and is *Ame-no-Mioya-Gami*, Japanese Father God. Different parts of El Cantare's core consciousness have descended to Earth in the past, once as Alpha and another as Elohim. His branch spirits, such as Shakyamuni Buddha and Hermes, have descended to Earth many times and helped to flourish many civilizations. To unite various religions and to integrate various fields of study in order to build a new civilization on Earth, a part of the core consciousness has descended to Earth as Master Ryuho Okawa.

Alpha is a part of the core consciousness of El Cantare who descended to Earth around 330 million years ago. Alpha preached Earth's Truths to harmonize and unify Earth-born humans and space people who came from other planets.

Elohim is a part of the core consciousness of El Cantare who descended to Earth around 150 million years ago. He gave wisdom, mainly on the differences of light and darkness, good and evil.

Ame-no-Mioya-Gami (Japanese Father God) is the Creator God and the Father God who appears in the ancient literature, *Hotsuma Tsutae*. It is believed that He descended on the foothills of Mt. Fuji about 30,000 years ago and built the Fuji dynasty, which is the root of the Japanese civilization. With justice as the central pillar, Ame-no-Mioya-Gami's teachings spread to ancient civilizations of other countries in the world.

Shakyamuni Buddha was born as a prince into the Shakya Clan in India around 2,600 years ago. When he was 29 years old, he renounced the world and sought enlightenment. He later attained Great Enlightenment and founded Buddhism.

Hermes is one of the 12 Olympian gods in Greek mythology, but the spiritual Truth is that he taught the teachings of love and progress around 4,300 years ago that became the origin of the current Western civilization. He is a hero that truly existed.

Ophealis was born in Greece around 6,500 years ago and was the leader who took an expedition to as far as Egypt. He is the God of miracles, prosperity, and arts, and is known as Osiris in the Egyptian mythology.

Rient Arl Croud was born as a king of the ancient Incan Empire around 7,000 years ago and taught about the mysteries of the mind. In the heavenly world, he is responsible for the interactions that take place between various planets.

Thoth was an almighty leader who built the golden age of the Atlantic civilization around 12,000 years ago. In the Egyptian mythology, he is known as God Thoth.

Ra Mu was a leader who built the golden age of the civilization of Mu around 17,000 years ago. As a religious leader and a politician, he ruled by uniting religion and politics.

ABOUT HAPPY SCIENCE

Happy Science is a religious group founded on the faith in El Cantare who is the God of the Earth, and the Creator of the universe. The essence of human beings is the soul that was created by God, and we all are children of God. God is our true parent, so in our souls we have a fundamental desire to "believe in God, love God, and get closer to God." And, we can get closer to God by living with God's Will as our own. In Happy Science, we call this the "Exploration of Right Mind." More specifically, it means to practice the Fourfold Path, which consists of "Love, Wisdom, Self-Reflection, and Progress."

Love: Love means "love that gives," or mercy. God hopes for the happiness of all people. Therefore, living with God's Will as our own means to start by practicing "love that gives."

Wisdom: By studying and putting spiritual knowledge into practice, you can cultivate wisdom and become better at resolving problems in life.

Self-Reflection: Once you learn the heart of God and the difference between His mind and yours, you should strive to bring your own mind closer to the mind of God—that process is called self-reflection. Self-reflection also includes meditation and prayer.

Progress: Since God hopes for the happiness of all people, you should also make progress in your love, and make an effort to realize utopia in which everyone in your society, country, and eventually all humankind can become happy.

As we practice this Fourfold Path, our souls will advance toward God step by step. That is when we can attain real happiness— our souls' desire to get closer to God comes true.

In Happy Science, we conduct activities to make ourselves happy through belief in Lord El Cantare, and to spread this faith to the world and bring happiness to all. We welcome you to join our activities!

We hold events and activities to help you practice the Fourfold Path at our branches, temples, missionary centers and missionary houses

Love: We hold various volunteering activities. Our members conduct missionary work together as the greatest practice of love.

Wisdom: We offer our comprehensive books collection, many of which are available online and at Happy Science locations. In addition, we give out numerous opportunities such as seminars or book clubs to learn the Truth.

Self-Reflection: We offer opportunities to polish your mind through self-reflection, meditation, and prayer. There are many cases in which members have experienced improvement in their human relationships by changing their own minds.

Progress: We also offer seminars to enhance your power of influence. Because it is also important to do well at work to make society better, we hold seminars to improve your work and management skills.

"The True Words Spoken By Buddha"

The True Words Spoken By Buddha is an English sutra given directly from the spirit of Shakyamuni Buddha, who is a part of Master Ryuho Okawa's subconscious. The words in this sutra are not of a mere human being but are the words of God or Buddha sent directly from the ninth dimension, which is the highest realm of the Earth's Spirit World.

    The True Words Spoken By Buddha is an essential sutra for us to connect and live with God or Buddha's Will as our own.

Miracles Brought by
"The True Words Spoken By Buddha"

Many Happy Science members have experienced miracles after reciting the sutra. Here, we will share some of them.

IIIIIIIIIIIIIIIIIIIIIIIIIIIIIIIIIIIIIIIIIIIIIIIIIIIIIIIIIIIIIIIIIIIIIIIIIIIIIIIIIIIIIIIIIIIIIIIIIIIIIIIIIIIIIII

A young girl resuscitated from cardiac arrest

A one-year-old girl in Peri Peri Village, Uganda, suffered cardiac arrest. After her father recited the sutra for 45 minutes, she was resuscitated. Her father said, "Any problem will be resolved if you have El Cantare Belief." "The Monument of Miracle" has been built to pass on the miraculous story.

My husband came back to life

"One day, I got a phone call informing me that my husband had a heart attack during his business trip. As I got on the bus and made my way to the hospital, I recited the sutra and prayed for his recovery. When I arrived, his heart no longer had problems. The doctor was confused, saying it was impossible. I am very thankful to the Lord."

(Mexico, 40s, Female)

The sutra dispelled an evil spirit

"I used to be an alcoholic. I suffered from recurrent sleep paralysis and nightmares of being murdered. Then, I recited the sutra three times a day—in the morning, at noon, and at night—and on the third morning, my shoulder and back suddenly felt much lighter. I felt as though I was freed from spiritual possession. I haven't experienced sleep paralysis and nightmares ever since." (Japan, 60s, Male)

MEMBERSHIPS

MEMBERSHIP

If you would like to know more about Happy Science, please consider becoming a member. Those who pledge to believe in Lord El Cantare and wish to learn more can join us.

When you become a member, you will receive the following sutra books: *The True Words Spoken By Buddha*, *Prayer to the Lord* and *Prayer to Guardian and Guiding Spirits*.

DEVOTEE MEMBER

If you would like to learn the teachings of Happy Science and walk the path of faith, become a Devotee member who pledges devotion to the Three Treasures, which are Buddha, Dharma, and Sangha. Buddha refers to Lord El Cantare, Master Ryuho Okawa. Dharma refers to Master Ryuho Okawa's teachings. Sangha refers to Happy Science. Devoting to the Three Treasures will let your Buddha nature shine, and you will enter the path to attain true freedom of the mind.

Becoming a devotee means you become Buddha's disciple. You will discipline your mind and act to bring happiness to society.

✉ EMAIL OR ☎ PHONE CALL
Please see the contact information page.

🔊 ONLINE [member.happy-science.org/signup/ 🔍]

A place to change your destiny—
Happy Science Branches

Since its establishment in 1986, Happy Science has been continuing its activities all over the world to create more people who can sincerely say, "I'm happy." We have more than 700 branches and temples around the world, where many people experience changes in their lives by connecting to God.

Good news—
My destiny changed for the better!

I was cured of my dysautonomia

"My fellow members at the branch suggested me to take seminars and recite the sutra many times. I did, and I was cured of my chronic dysautonomia!"　　(60s, Female)

Positive thinking cured me of my rheumatism

"My colleague introduced me to Happy Science when I was sick. After I reflected on my self-deprecating tendency and took a ritual prayer, my rheumatism disappeared and my test results showed acceptable values."
(50s, Female)

I want to convey the Truth to my friends

"I felt reassured when I learned that we can strengthen our immunity and repel the coronavirus through faith in El Cantare. Many friends my age fear being infected by the virus, so I want to convey Master's Truth to let them know there's nothing to fear."　　(80s, Male)

My relationship with others improved

"My tendency to be strict on others often led me to trouble with my coworkers. But after consulting my branch manager, who advised me to refine my mind, I could improve my relationship with my coworkers as I did not judge them as much as I did before."　　(30s, Male)

CONTACT INFORMATION

Happy Science is a worldwide organization with branches and temples around the globe. For a comprehensive list, visit the worldwide directory at happy-science.org. The following are some of our main Happy Science locations:

UNITED STATES AND CANADA

New York
79 Franklin St., New York, NY 10013, USA
Phone: 1-212-343-7972
Fax: 1-212-343-7973
Email: ny@happy-science.org
Website: happyscience-usa.org

New Jersey
66 Hudson St., #2R, Hoboken, NJ 07030, USA
Phone: 1-201-313-0127
Email: nj@happy-science.org
Website: happyscience-usa.org

Chicago
2300 Barrington Rd., Suite #400,
Hoffman Estates, IL 60169, USA
Phone: 1-630-937-3077
Email: chicago@happy-science.org
Website: happyscience-usa.org

Florida
5208 8th St., Zephyrhills, FL 33542, USA
Phone: 1-813-715-0000
Fax: 1-813-715-0010
Email: florida@happy-science.org
Website: happyscience-usa.org

Atlanta
1874 Piedmont Ave., NE Suite 360-C
Atlanta, GA 30324, USA
Phone: 1-404-892-7770
Email: atlanta@happy-science.org
Website: happyscience-usa.org

San Francisco
525 Clinton St.
Redwood City, CA 94062, USA
Phone & Fax: 1-650-363-2777
Email: sf@happy-science.org
Website: happyscience-usa.org

Los Angeles
1590 E. Del Mar Blvd., Pasadena,
CA 91106, USA
Phone: 1-626-395-7775
Fax: 1-626-395-7776
Email: la@happy-science.org
Website: happyscience-usa.org

Orange County
16541 Gothard St. Suite 104
Huntington Beach, CA 92647
Phone: 1-714-659-1501
Email: oc@happy-science.org
Website: happyscience-usa.org

San Diego
7841 Balboa Ave. Suite #202
San Diego, CA 92111, USA
Phone: 1-626-395-7775
Fax: 1-626-395-7776
E-mail: sandiego@happy-science.org
Website: happyscience-usa.org

Hawaii
Phone: 1-808-591-9772
Fax: 1-808-591-9776
Email: hi@happy-science.org
Website: happyscience-usa.org

Kauai
3343 Kanakolu Street, Suite 5
Lihue, HI 96766, USA
Phone: 1-808-822-7007
Fax: 1-808-822-6007
Email: kauai-hi@happy-science.org
Website: happyscience-usa.org

Toronto

845 The Queensway
Etobicoke, ON M8Z 1N6, Canada
Phone: 1-416-901-3747
Email: toronto@happy-science.org
Website: happy-science.ca

Vancouver

#201-2607 East 49th Avenue,
Vancouver, BC, V5S 1J9, Canada
Phone: 1-604-437-7735
Fax: 1-604-437-7764
Email: vancouver@happy-science.org
Website: happy-science.ca

INTERNATIONAL

Tokyo

1-6-7 Togoshi, Shinagawa,
Tokyo, 142-0041, Japan
Phone: 81-3-6384-5770
Fax: 81-3-6384-5776
Email: tokyo@happy-science.org
Website: happy-science.org

London

3 Margaret St.
London, W1W 8RE United Kingdom
Phone: 44-20-7323-9255
Fax: 44-20-7323-9344
Email: eu@happy-science.org
Website: www.happyscience-uk.org

Sydney

516 Pacific Highway, Lane Cove North,
2066 NSW, Australia
Phone: 61-2-9411-2877
Fax: 61-2-9411-2822
Email: sydney@happy-science.org

Sao Paulo

Rua. Domingos de Morais 1154,
Vila Mariana, Sao Paulo SP
CEP 04010-100, Brazil
Phone: 55-11-5088-3800
Email: sp@happy-science.org
Website: happyscience.com.br

Jundiai

Rua Congo, 447, Jd. Bonfiglioli
Jundiai-CEP, 13207-340, Brazil
Phone: 55-11-4587-5952
Email: jundiai@happy-science.org

Seoul

74, Sadang-ro 27-gil,
Dongjak-gu, Seoul, Korea
Phone: 82-2-3478-8777
Fax: 82-2-3478-9777
Email: korea@happy-science.org

Taipei

No. 89, Lane 155, Dunhua N. Road,
Songshan District, Taipei City 105, Taiwan
Phone: 886-2-2719-9377
Fax: 886-2-2719-5570
Email: taiwan@happy-science.org

Taichung

No. 146, Minzu Rd., Central Dist.,
Taichung City 400001, Taiwan
Phone: 886-4-22233777
Email: taichung@happy-science.org

Kuala Lumpur

No 22A, Block 2, Jalil Link Jalan Jalil Jaya
2, Bukit Jalil 57000,
Kuala Lumpur, Malaysia
Phone: 60-3-8998-7877
Fax: 60-3-8998-7977
Email: malaysia@happy-science.org
Website: happyscience.org.my

Kathmandu

Kathmandu Metropolitan City,
Ward No. 15, Ring Road, Kimdol,
Sitapaila Kathmandu, Nepal
Phone: 977-1-537-2931
Email: nepal@happy-science.org

Kampala

Plot 877 Rubaga Road, Kampala
P.O. Box 34130 Kampala, UGANDA
Email: uganda@happy-science.org

ABOUT IRH PRESS USA

IRH Press USA Inc. was founded in 2013 as an affiliated firm of IRH Press Co., Ltd., based in New York. The press exclusively publishes comprehensive titles by Ryuho Okawa, an international bestselling author who has written more than 3,100 titles on Self-Improvement, Spiritual Truth, Religious Truth and more, with 100 million copies sold worldwide. For more information, visit okawabooks.com.

Follow us on:

f Facebook: Okawa Books   Instagram: OkawaBooks

▶ Youtube: Okawa Books   Twitter: Okawa Books

𝓟 Pinterest: Okawa Books   **g** Goodreads: Ryuho Okawa

———— **NEWSLETTER** ————

To receive book related news, promotions and events, please subscribe to our newsletter below.

🔗 irhpress.com/pages/subscribe

———— **AUDIO / VISUAL MEDIA** ————

YOUTUBE   **PODCAST**

Introduction of Ryuho Okawa's titles; topics ranging from self-help, current affairs, spirituality, religion, and the universe.